Wonders

Reading/Writing Companion

McGraw Hill

mheducation.com/prek-12

Send all inquiries to:
McGraw Hill
1325 Avenue of the Americas
New York, NY 10019

ISBN: 978-1-26-575493-8
MHID: 1-26-575493-4

Printed in the United States of America.

1 2 3 4 5 6 7 8 9 LMN 26 25 24 23 22 21   A

Welcome to
WONDERS!

We're here to help you set goals to build on the amazing things you already know. We'll also help you reflect on everything you'll learn.

Let's start by taking a look at the incredible things you'll do this year.

You'll build knowledge on exciting topics and find answers to interesting questions.

You'll read fascinating fiction, informational texts, and poetry and respond to what you read with your own thoughts and ideas.

And you'll research and write stories, poems, and essays of your own!

Here's a sneak peek at how you'll do it all.

"Let's go!"

You'll explore new ideas by reading groups of different texts about the same topic. These groups of texts are called *text sets*.

At the beginning of a text set, we'll help you set goals on the My Goals page. You'll see a bar with four boxes beneath each goal. Think about what you already know to fill in the bar. Here's an example.

I can read and understand narrative nonfiction.

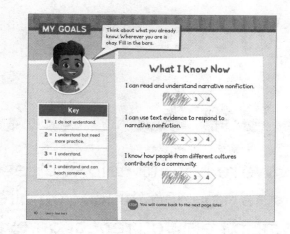

As you move through a text set, you'll explore an essential question and build your knowledge of a topic until you're ready to write about it yourself.

You'll also learn skills that will help you reach your text set goals. At the end of lessons, you'll see a new Check In bar with four boxes.

CHECK IN 1 2 3 4

Reflect on how well you understood a lesson to fill in the bar.

Here are some questions you can ask yourself.

• Was I able to complete the task?

• Was it easy, or was it hard?

• Do I think I need more practice?

You have plenty of tools and resources to learn more, such as anchor charts and center activities. You can also reread a lesson or ask a teacher or peer for help.

It's okay if I think I need more practice. The most important thing is that I do my best and keep learning!

Thinking about what works best for me will help me choose what to do next.

At the end of each text set, you'll show off the knowledge you built by completing a fun task. Then you'll return to the second My Goals page where we'll help you reflect on all that you learned.

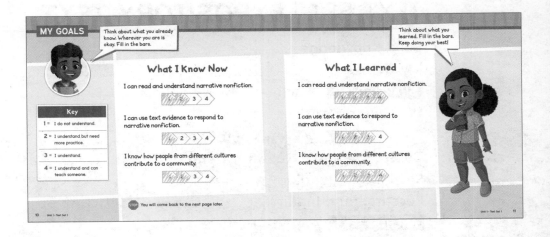

I'll fill in a new set of bars to show how far I've come. I started at 2, but now I'm at 4 because I can read and understand narrative nonfiction well enough to teach a friend.

I'll follow the same steps as I write my own stories, essays, and poems. I own my learning, and you can own yours!

"Let's get started!"

TEXT SET 1 **EXPOSITORY TEXT**

TEXT SET 2 **FOLKTALE**

TEXT SET 3 **EXPOSITORY TEXT**

EXTENDED WRITING

CONNECT AND REFLECT

Digital Tools
Find this eBook and
other resources at
my.mheducation.com

Peter Mah/iStockphoto/Getty Images

TEXT SET 1 **REALISTIC FICTION**

TEXT SET 2 **EXPOSITORY TEXT**

TEXT SET 3 **POETRY**

EXTENDED WRITING

CONNECT AND REFLECT

Digital Tools

Find this eBook and
other resources at
my.mheducation.com

Diverse Images/Universal Images Group/Getty Images

Build Knowledge

? **Essential Question**

What do we know about Earth and its neighbors?

Build Vocabulary

Write new words you learned about Earth and the solar system. Draw lines and circles for the words you write.

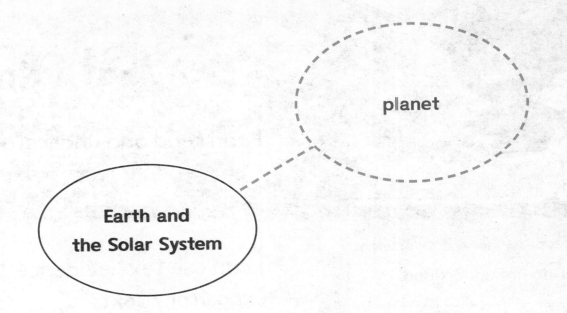

planet

Earth and
the Solar System

Go online to **my.mheducation.com** and read the "Eyes in the Sky" Blast. Think about why learning about satellites is important. Then blast back your response.

Think about what you already know. Fill in the bars. This will be a good start.

What I Know Now

I can read and understand expository text.

1 > 2 > 3 > 4

I can use text evidence to respond to expository text.

1 > 2 > 3 > 4

I know how we learn about Earth and its neighbors.

1 > 2 > 3 > 4

Key	
1 =	I do not understand.
2 =	I understand but need more practice.
3 =	I understand.
4 =	I understand and can teach someone.

STOP You will come back to the next page later.

> Think about what you learned.
> Fill in the bars. What are you getting better at?

What I Learned

I can read and understand expository text.

I can use text evidence to respond to expository text.

I know how we learn about Earth and its neighbors.

1 > 2 > 3 > 4

My Goal I can read and understand expository text.

TAKE NOTES

As you read, make note of interesting words and important information.

Earth and its neighbors

Essential Question

? What do we know about Earth and its neighbors?

Read about how we have learned about space.

Galileo studied the sky with a telescope he built.

(bkgd)Ian McKinnell/Photographer's Choice/Getty Images; Sarin Images/The Granger Collection, NYC

If the Sun could talk, it might say, "Look at me! Look at my sunspots! I am so hot!" Without the Sun, Earth would be a cold, dark planet. How do we know this?

Thanks to the astronomer Galileo, we know a lot about the Sun and the rest of our **solar system**.

Telescopes: Looking Up

Galileo did not invent the telescope. However, 400 years ago he did build one that was strong enough to study the sky. When Galileo looked into space, he saw the rocky **surface** of the Moon. When he looked at the Sun, he discovered spots on its fiery surface.

The Moon is Earth's closest neighbor.

StockTrek/Photodisc/Getty Images

FIND TEXT EVIDENCE

> Read

Paragraphs 1–2
Summarize
What did Galileo study?

_____

_____

Circle text evidence.

Paragraph 3
Central Idea and Details
Underline details that describe what Galileo saw. What is the central idea of this section?

_____

_____

_____

_____

> Reread

Author's Craft

How does the author help you see what an astronomer sees?

FIND TEXT EVIDENCE 🔍

Read

Paragraph 1
Key Words
Circle the key word in the first sentence. What does it mean?

_____

_____

Paragraphs 2–4
Central Idea and Details
Underline relevant details about satellites. What is the central idea of this section?

_____

_____

_____

_____

_____

Reread

Author's Craft

How does the author help you understand what satellites do?

Astronomy, or the study of space, began with the simple telescope. But astronomers wanted to look at the sky more closely. They made bigger telescopes that could see farther than the one Galileo used. Astronomers still had many questions.

Satellites: A Step Closer

In 1958, scientists launched Explorer 1, the first American satellite, into space. It was an exciting day for America.

Soon many satellites circled the **globe** and took photographs of Earth, the Moon, stars, and other planets. They collected a large **amount** of information. Satellites even tracked the **temperature** on the planet Saturn.

Explorer 1 takes off.

Scientists have learned many things about the solar system from satellites. That's why they kept sending more into space. Soon there were hundreds of satellites in space making amazing discoveries, but astronomers wanted to know even more. That's why they found a way to put a man on the Moon.

(bkgd)NASA, ESA, R. OConnell (University of Virginia), and the Hubble Heritage Team (STScI/AURA), NASA Marshall Space Flight Center (NASA-MSFC)

One Giant Leap

On April 12, 1961, Russian cosmonaut Yuri Gagarin became the first man to travel into space. Just 23 days later, American **astronaut** Alan Shepard followed. Both flights were short, but they proved that people could go into space.

After Shepard, more astronauts went into space. Some orbited Earth. Some walked on the dusty, bumpy surface of the Moon. They took pictures and collected Moon rocks. Astronauts wanted to answer some important questions. Did the Sun's **warmth** heat the Moon? Could the Moon **support** life someday?

Astronaut Edwin "Buzz" Aldrin walks toward the lunar module. Aldrin left his footprints on the Moon.

Aldrin brought home this Moon rock.

(bl)MPI/Archive Photos/Getty Images, (br)NASA Johnson Space Center (NASA-JSC)

FIND TEXT EVIDENCE

Read

Paragraph 1

Summarize

Why was 1961 an important year for space exploration? Summarize in your own words.

_____

_____

Underline text evidence.

Paragraph 2

Suffixes

Circle two words that describe the surface of the Moon. Write what they mean here.

_____

_____

Reread

Author's Craft

Why is "One Giant Leap" a good heading for this section?

FIND TEXT EVIDENCE

Read

Paragraph 1

Summarize

Draw a box around details that show what scientists did. Summarize in your own words.

_____

_____

_____

Paragraph 2

Central Idea and Details

Underline relevant details that tell you about the Hubble Space Telescope. What is the central idea of this section?

_____

_____

_____

_____

Scientists studied the photographs and Moon rocks that the astronauts brought back. They made exciting discoveries using telescopes and satellites. But it wasn't enough. Scientists wanted to get closer to the other planets. Soon they found a way!

Hubble and Beyond

Scientists created another telescope, but this time it was gigantic. They sent it up into space. The Hubble Space Telescope was launched in 1990. It's still up there and orbits Earth above the clouds. It takes clear, close-up photographs of stars and planets. It sends fascinating information back to Earth. The Hubble helps scientists study Earth and its neighbors. It also helps astronomers see planets outside our solar system.

It takes the Hubble Telescope 96 minutes to orbit Earth.

Frank Whitney/The Image Bank/Getty Images

More Discoveries Every Day

Scientists are still asking questions about Earth and its neighbors in space. With the help of satellites, telescopes, and astronauts, they will continue to **explore** and find answers.

What Can We See?

With Our Eyes	With a Simple Telescope	With the Hubble Telescope
The Moon	Craters on the moon	Planets outside our solar system
The Sun	Sunspots	Stars bigger than the Sun and farther away
Mars	Clouds around Jupiter	Jupiter's surface

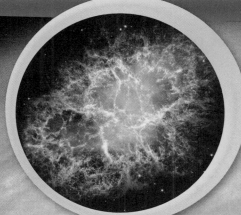

This is a Hubble Telescope photo of an exploding star.

Summarize

Use your notes to summarize "Earth and Its Neighbors" using the text's central idea and relevant details.

FIND TEXT EVIDENCE

Read

Paragraph 1

Key Words

Circle the word *explore*. Write an interesting detail about it.

_____

_____

Page 17

Charts

Underline three things you can see with the Hubble Telescope.

List three things you can see with your eyes.

_____

_____

_____

Reread

Author's Craft

How does the author use key words to help you understand more about space?

Vocabulary

Use the sentences to talk with a partner about each word. Then answer the questions.

amount

James drank a small **amount** of water.

What could you use to carry a large amount of water?

_____

astronomy

Kia studied **astronomy** to learn more about stars.

What could you learn about by studying astronomy?

_____

globe

Earth is a big, round **globe**.

What is another word for *globe*?

_____

_____

solar system

Mercury is one of the planets in our **solar system**.

What is at the center of our solar system?

_____

_____

support

My dad and I **support** our favorite baseball team by cheering.

What can you do to show your support?

_____

_____

Build Your Word List Draw a box around the word *simple* on page 14. In your reader's notebook, use a word web to write words that mean almost the same thing. Use a dictionary to help you.

surface

The **surface** of the Moon is dry and dusty.

Describe the surface of your desk.

_____

_____

temperature

We can have fun even when the **temperature** outside is cold.

What is the temperature where you are today?

_____

_____

warmth

Will and Paul cooked marshmallows over the **warmth** of a fire.

What is another word for *warmth*?

_____

_____

Suffixes

A suffix is a word part added to the end of a word. It changes the word's meaning. The suffix *-y* means "full of." The suffix *-ly* means "in a certain way."

🔍 FIND TEXT EVIDENCE

On page 13 in "Earth and Its Neighbors," I see the word rocky. Rocky *has the suffix -y. I know that the suffix -y means "full of." The word* rocky *must mean "full of rocks."*

When Galileo looked into space, he saw the rocky surface of the Moon.

Your Turn Find the suffix in the word below. Use it to figure out the word's meaning.

closely, page 14 _____

_____

_____

CHECK IN ⟩ 1 ⟩ 2 ⟩ 3 ⟩ 4 ⟩

Sarin Images/The Granger Collection, NYC

Summarize

When you summarize an expository text, you state the central idea and relevant details of each section. It's important to paraphrase, or use your own words, when you summarize.

🔍 FIND TEXT EVIDENCE

How did telescopes help us learn about space? Find the central idea and relevant details. Summarize them in your own words.

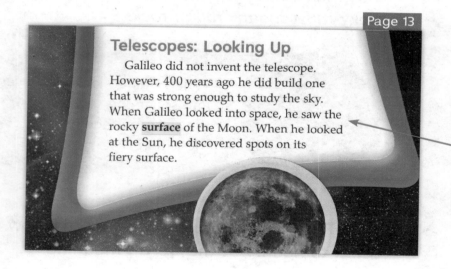

Page 13

Telescopes: Looking Up

Galileo did not invent the telescope. However, 400 years ago he did build one that was strong enough to study the sky. When Galileo looked into space, he saw the rocky **surface** of the Moon. When he looked at the Sun, he discovered spots on its fiery surface.

I read that Galileo built a telescope. He discovered sunspots and saw the Moon's surface. Details help me summarize. Telescopes helped scientists learn more about space.

Your Turn Reread "Satellites: A Step Closer" on page 14. Think about the central idea and relevant details in this section. Then summarize the section here.

_____

_____

CHECK IN 1 > 2 > 3 > 4

Key Words and Charts

"Earth and Its Neighbors" is an **expository text**. Expository text

- gives facts and information about a topic
- has text features, such as headings, key words, and charts, that support the author's purpose

FIND TEXT EVIDENCE

I can tell that "Earth and Its Neighbors" is an expository text. It gives facts and information about telescopes, satellites, and space. It has headings, key words, and a chart.

Readers to Writers

An author's purpose for writing an expository text is to inform. When you write an expository text, consider using a chart to help your readers compare information and better understand your topic.

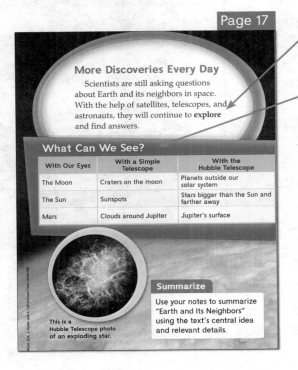

Page 17

More Discoveries Every Day

Scientists are still asking questions about Earth and its neighbors in space. With the help of satellites, telescopes, and astronauts, they will continue to **explore** and find answers.

What Can We See?

With Our Eyes	With a Simple Telescope	With the Hubble Telescope
The Moon	Craters on the moon	Planets outside our solar system
The Sun	Sunspots	Stars bigger than the Sun and farther away
Mars	Clouds around Jupiter	Jupiter's surface

Summarize

Use your notes to summarize "Earth and Its Neighbors" using the text's central idea and relevant details.

This is a Hubble Telescope photo of an exploding star.

Key Words
Key words are important words related to the topic.

Charts
A chart is a list of facts arranged in rows and columns. It helps readers compare information.

Your Turn Look at the chart on page 17. Write one way the Hubble Telescope is different from a simple telescope.

_____

_____

_____

CHECK IN 1 2 3 4

Central Idea and Relevant Details

The central, or main, idea is the most important point an author makes about a topic. Relevant details support the central idea.

🔍 **FIND TEXT EVIDENCE**

I can reread the first paragraph on page 14 and look for details that are relevant to the topic. Then I can think about what these details have in common to figure out the central idea.

Quick Tip

Remember that you can use text features, such as headings and key words, to help you figure out the topic of a section of text.

Central Idea
Astronomers are always searching for new tools that will help them better study space.

Detail
Astronomers wanted to look at the sky more closely.

Detail
They made bigger telescopes that could see farther than the one Galileo used.

Detail
Astronomy, the study of space, began with a simple telescope.

 Your Turn Reread "One Giant Leap" on pages 15 and 16. Find relevant details that tell you about astronauts. List them in your graphic organizer. Use the details to figure out the central idea.

CHECK IN 1 ⟩ 2 ⟩ 3 ⟩ 4

Central Idea
Detail
Detail
Detail

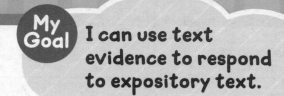

Respond to Reading

Talk about the prompt below. Use your notes and evidence from the text to support your answer.

Why do scientists want to find new and better ways to explore Earth and its neighbors?

_____

_____

_____

_____

_____

_____

_____

_____

_____

_____

_____

Quick Tip

Use these sentence starters to talk about the prompt.

The author explains . . .

Scientists want to find better ways to explore space because . . .

Grammar Connections

As you write your response, be sure to use commas to separate items in a list.

CHECK IN 1 > 2 > 3 > 4 >

The Sun and Stars

COLLABORATE

People have observed and studied stars for thousands of years. The star closest to Earth is the Sun. Follow the research process to learn more about the Sun and other stars. Then write about what you've learned in a genre of your choice. Work with a partner.

Step 1 **Set a Goal** Choose a genre to present your information. You can choose an expository essay, opinion essay, fictional story, poem, or something else.

Step 2 **Identify Sources** Use reliable books, encyclopedias, videos, or websites to learn about the Sun and stars.

Step 3 **Find and Record Information** Take notes on your sources by paraphrasing, or writing information in your own words. You can find information about different kinds of stars, why some stars look bigger or brighter than others, and what stars are made of.

Step 4 **Organize and Combine Information** Review your notes. Choose which facts you would like to include in your writing. Make an outline or story map of what you will write.

Step 5 **Create and Present** Write your essay, story, or poem. Add a Works Cited page, or list of sources you used for research. Then share your writing with your class.

Quick Tip

It's important to give credit to your sources. Avoid plagiarism, or copying an author's exact words and using them as your own. Cite your sources in a Works Cited page. This is an alphabetical list of sources with each source's author, title, and publication information.

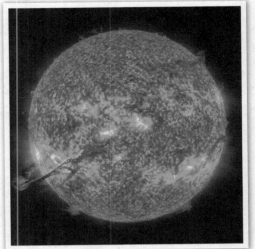

NASA/GSFC/SDO

CHECK IN ⟩ 1 ⟩ 2 ⟩ 3 ⟩ 4

Literature Anthology:
pages 194–207

Earth

? How do the diagrams and labels help you understand more about the solar system?

COLLABORATE

Talk About It Look at the diagram on **Literature Anthology** pages 198 and 199. Talk with a partner about what the diagram helps you understand.

Cite Text Evidence Why does the author include text features, such as a diagram, heading, and caption? Tell why in the chart.

Text Feature	How It Helps

Write The author uses text features to help me _____

_____

CHECK IN ⟩ 1 ⟩ 2 ⟩ 3 ⟩ 4

Quick Tip

Pay careful attention to text features in an expository text. Headings often state the central idea of a section of text. Captions and diagrams add more information. Use these features to better understand the topic.

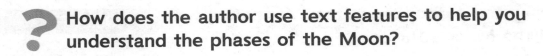

? How does the author use text features to help you understand the phases of the Moon?

COLLABORATE

Talk About It Reread **Literature Anthology** page 204. Talk with a partner about how the diagram explains the Moon's phases.

Cite Text Evidence How do the text, diagram, and caption work together to help you understand the phases of the Moon? Use the chart to record evidence.

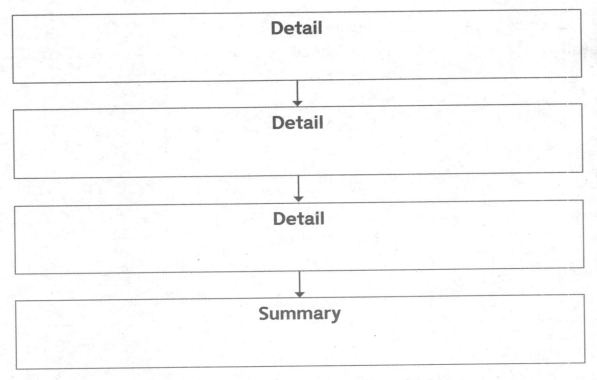

| Detail |
| Detail |
| Detail |
| Summary |

Write The text and caption explain _____

_____

CHECK IN 1 2 3 4

? **How does the way the author organizes information help you understand the Moon's surface?**

Talk About It Reread **Literature Anthology** page 206. Describe to a partner what the surface of the Moon looks like.

Cite Text Evidence How does the author organize the information about the Moon's surface? Write evidence in the chart and explain how it helps you understand the topic.

Quick Tip

You can use images to visualize the text. You can use captions to learn more about the images.

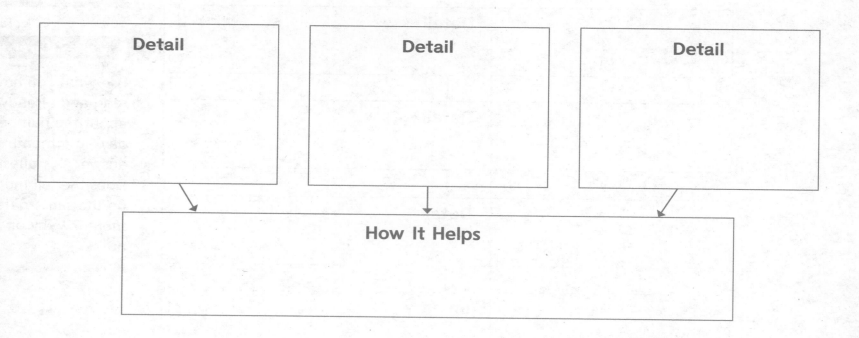

Detail

Detail

Detail

How It Helps

Write I understand about the Moon's surface because the author

_____

_____

CHECK IN 1 2 3 4

Respond to Reading

COLLABORATE

Talk about the prompt below. Use your notes and evidence from the text to support your answer.

Describe the relationship between Earth, the Moon, and their neighboring planets.

_____

_____

_____

_____

_____

_____

_____

_____

_____

Quick Tip

Use these sentence starters to talk about the prompt.

In Earth, Jeffrey Zuehlke explains . . .

Diagrams and photographs show . . .

This helps me understand . . .

CHECK IN 1 〉 2 〉 3 〉 4 〉

Why the Sun Is Red

Literature Anthology:
pages 210–211

1   "I'm wondering," said the King to his horseman, while pointing to the rosy sunset. "Why is the Sun red while setting and rising, but yellow the rest of the day?"

2   "Perhaps it's not for us to know," said the horseman.

3   "The Sun's mother must know," said the King. "You're just the one to find her, in her amber house. Its surface glows bright orange. If you find the answer to my question, I'll fill your hat with gold!" said the King. "But if you don't, you must leave my kingdom forever."

4   For seven days the horseman searched. Then, one rainy evening, he saw a glow. It was the amber house! An old woman opened the door. It was the Sun's mother.

Reread and use the prompts to take notes in the text.

Reread paragraphs 1–3. **Underline** the King's question. Write how the horseman will find the answer for the King.

_____

_____

_____

Reread paragraph 4. **Circle** the clues that show that the horseman has found the Sun's mother.

COLLABORATE

Reread paragraphs 2–4. Discuss how the horseman feels about being sent to answer the King's question. **Draw a box around** text evidence that helps you understand how the horseman feels.

1   The Sun returned, and the mother said, "A man was here. He wished to know why you're red when you rise and set, but yellow the rest of the day."

2   "How dare he ask!" shouted the Sun.

3   "He left," said her mother. "But why are you angry? It's a simple question."

4   "I'm angry because every morning and evening I draw near the sea and see her," said the Sun.

5   "Her?"

6   "She is the most beautiful princess in the world. She makes me red with envy."

7   The horseman had his answer. He sped away on his horse.

8   The pleased King had his answer. He filled the horseman's hat with gold. The horseman bowed and left quickly, eager for the warmth of his own bed.

Reread paragraphs 1-6. **Circle** evidence that shows how the Sun feels. Describe how she feels in your own words.

_____

_____

_____

_____

COLLABORATE

Reread paragraphs 7 and 8. **Underline** phrases that help you visualize what happens after the King gives the horseman the gold. Talk with a partner about how visualizing what the horseman does helps you understand how he feels.

Remember to listen actively to your partner. Ask questions that have to do with understanding how the horseman feels. Make comments that stick to the topic you are discussing.

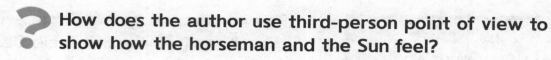

? How does the author use third-person point of view to show how the horseman and the Sun feel?

COLLABORATE

Talk About It Reread the selection on pages 30 and 31. Discuss what the author does to show how the characters feel.

Cite Text Evidence What text evidence helps you understand how the horseman and the Sun feel?

The Horseman	The Sun

Write I know how the characters feel because the author

_____

_____

CHECK IN 1 2 3 4

Personification

Personification refers to when an author gives human qualities or actions to a thing or idea. Personification is a kind of figurative language. *The Sun pushed aside the dark clouds* is an example of personification. The Sun cannot actually push something as a person can. This is figurative language to explain and help the reader visualize the weather.

🔍 FIND TEXT EVIDENCE

In "Why the Sun Is Red," the Sun is represented as a person to explain something in nature. One example of this is on page 30, when the King says the Sun has a mother.

> "The Sun's mother must know," said the King.

Your Turn Reread paragraphs 1–6 on page 31.

- What is another example of the author representing the Sun as a person? _____

  _____

- Why do you think the author gives human feelings and actions to the Sun? _____

  _____

Personification can make your writing more interesting to read. As you draft and revise your own writing, think of how you can give a human action, such as dancing, leaping, or smiling, to an object or idea.

CHECK IN ⟩ 1 ⟩ 2 ⟩ 3 ⟩ 4 ⟩

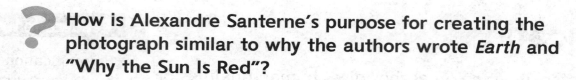

? **How is Alexandre Santerne's purpose for creating the photograph similar to why the authors wrote *Earth* and "Why the Sun Is Red"?**

COLLABORATE

Talk About It Discuss what you see in the photograph. Read the caption and talk about why the stars look like trails.

Cite Text Evidence **Circle** clues in the photograph that help you understand how Earth moves. Then reread the caption and underline how Alexandre Santerne created the photograph.

Write The authors' purposes are like the photographer's purpose

because _____

_____

_____

_____

_____

_____

This photograph is called "Star Trails over La Silla." To create it, photographer Alexandre Santerne took many pictures of the stars at night. Then he combined all of the photos into one. The stars look like trails because of Earth's rotation.

CHECK IN 〉 1 〉 2 〉 3 〉 4

Write an Astronaut's Journal

Think over what you learned about space exploration. Why do you think it's important for humans to explore space and learn about the solar system? Use text evidence to support your ideas.

1. Look at your Build Knowledge notes in your reader's notebook.

2. Write a journal entry from the perspective of an astronaut exploring space. Describe what you might see and experience in space. Include some ideas about why learning about space is important. Use some of the new vocabulary words you learned in your writing.

3. Include drawings to go along with your journal entry. What might an astronaut see outside the window of a spaceship?

Think about what you learned in this text set. Fill in the bars on page 11.

Build Knowledge

Essential Question

What makes different animals unique?

Build Vocabulary

Write new words you learned about animals and what makes them unique. Draw lines and circles for the words you write.

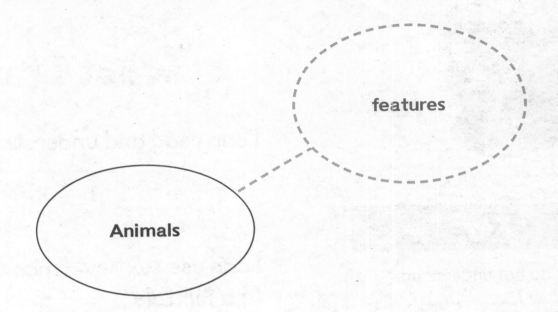

features

Animals

Go online to **my.mheducation.com** and read the Blast titled "The Perfect Predator." Think about why learning about animals is important. Then blast back your response.

MY GOALS

Think about what you already know. Fill in the bars. It's okay if you want more practice.

What I Know Now

I can read and understand a folktale.

I can use text evidence to respond to a folktale.

I know what makes different animals unique.

1 > 2 > 3 > 4

STOP You will come back to the next page later.

Think about what you learned. Fill in the bars. What progress did you make?

What I Learned

I can read and understand a folktale.

1 > 2 > 3 > 4

I can use text evidence to respond to a folktale.

1 > 2 > 3 > 4

I know what makes different animals unique.

1 > 2 > 3 > 4

My Goal I can read and understand a folktale.

TAKE NOTES

As you read, make note of interesting words and important events.

Anansi
Learns a Lesson

Essential Question

?

What makes different animals unique?

Read about how Turtle solves his problem.

Anansi the Spider loved to play tricks on his friends. One afternoon, Turtle stopped by as Anansi was making lunch.

"I hate to bother you as you get ready to eat your meal, but those bananas look **splendid**," said the shy Turtle. "I am so hungry."

Anansi was careful and kept a **watchful** eye on this food. He didn't want to share his lunch. So he decided to play a trick on Turtle.

"Please, help yourself," Anansi said with a sly and tricky grin as he **offered** Turtle some food.

FIND TEXT EVIDENCE 🔍

> Read

Paragraphs 1–2
Character Perspective
How does Turtle feel when he first sees Anansi?

_____

_____

Underline the text evidence.

Paragraph 3
Visualize
Draw a box around words or phrases that help you visualize, or picture, what Anansi is like.

Paragraph 4
Synonyms
Circle a synonym for the word _sly_. Write what _sly_ means here.

_____

> Reread

Author's Craft

How does dialogue help you understand what Turtle is like?

FIND TEXT EVIDENCE 🔍

Read

Paragraphs 1–5
Visualize
Underline text that helps you picture how Anansi keeps Turtle from eating the bananas.

Paragraph 6
Character Perspective
How does Turtle feel when Anansi asks him to wash his hands again?

_____

_____

Draw a box around text that supports your answer.

Paragraph 7
Theme
Circle evidence that reveals what Anansi did to Turtle.

Reread

Author's Craft

How does the author help you understand why Turtle is upset?

Turtle reached for the food. "Aren't you going to wash your hands first?" asked Anansi.

"Oh, yes!" Turtle said. When Turtle returned, Anansi had eaten half of the bananas.

"I didn't want the bananas to spoil," said Anansi.

Turtle got closer and made another attempt to eat. Anansi stared at Turtle in **disbelief**.

"Turtle, please wash your hands again," he said.

Turtle was upset and filled with **dismay**. He knew his hands were clean, but he went to wash them again. When he returned Anansi had eaten all of the fruit.

"Ha, ha, I tricked you, Turtle," said Anansi. "You didn't get any bananas!"

Turtle was angry that Anansi had tricked him. But he was also tricky and clever. These were two of his best **features**. He decided to play a little trick on his friend.

"Please come to my house at the bottom of the lake for a **fabulous** feast tomorrow," said Turtle. Anansi quickly said yes to the meal.

Turtle decided to ask Fish to help. "Fish, I want to play a little trick on Anansi," he said. "Will you help?"

Fish agreed, and together the two friends created a **unique**, or one of a kind, plan.

FIND TEXT EVIDENCE 🔍

Read

Paragraph 1
Character Perspective
How does Turtle feel about Anansi's trick? What does he decide to do?

_____

_____

Circle text evidence.

Paragraph 2
Synonyms
Draw a box around the synonym for *feast*.

Paragraphs 2–4
Make Inferences
Use what Turtle says to make an inference about how he will trick Anansi. Write it here.

_____

_____

_____

FIND TEXT EVIDENCE

Read

Paragraphs 1–3

Character Perspective

How does Anansi feel when he meets Fish at the lake? Why does he feel this way?

_____

_____

_____

_____

Underline text evidence that supports your answer.

Paragraph 4

Visualize

Draw a box around text that helps you visualize what Anansi finds at Turtle's house.

Reread

Author's Craft

How does the author use repetition to help you understand what _sank_ means?

The next day, Fish met Anansi at the edge of the lake. "Come, Anansi," said Fish. "We will swim to Turtle's house together." Anansi looked at the water. He was an awkward and clumsy swimmer. He was also very light.

"How will I ever get down to Turtle's house?" he cried.

"Grab some heavy stones," said Fish. "Then you will be heavy enough to sink."

Anansi picked up two big stones, jumped into the lake, and sank down, down, down. At Turtle's house, Anansi saw a wonderful feast of berries.

"Welcome, Anansi," said Turtle. "Drop those stones and help yourself."

As soon as Anansi dropped the stones, he rocketed to the surface of the lake. Anansi sputtered furiously. "Fish and Turtle tricked me," he cried angrily.

Back at the bottom of the lake, Turtle and Fish laughed and laughed.

"Anansi has tricked us many times," said Turtle. "For once, we tricked him."

Summarize

Look at your notes and think about what happens in "Anansi Learns a Lesson." Use the theme and plot events to summarize the text.

FIND TEXT EVIDENCE

Read

Paragraphs 1–4

Visualize

Underline text that helps you picture what happens to Anansi when he drops the stones.

Character Perspective

How does Anansi react to Fish and Turtle's trick?

_____

_____

Circle text evidence.

Theme

What lesson does Anansi learn?

_____

_____

Reread

Author's Craft

How does the author help you understand how Turtle and Fish feel about tricking Anansi?

Vocabulary

Use the sentences to talk with a partner about each word. Then answer the questions.

disbelief

Winnie stared in **disbelief** at the huge shark.

What is something that would make you stare in disbelief?

_____

_____

dismay

Marco looked at the rain with sadness and **dismay**.

Describe a time when you felt dismay.

_____

_____

> **Build Your Word List** Choose one of the interesting words you noted on page 40. Create a word web with related forms of the word in your reader's notebook.

fabulous

The fireworks were amazing and **fabulous**.

What do you think is fabulous?

_____

_____

features

My kitten's pink nose is one of its cutest **features**.

What is one of your best features?

_____

_____

offered

Jayden **offered** to help Mia pick up her books.

How has someone offered to help you?

_____

_____

splendid

Katie's day at the zoo ended with a wonderful, **splendid** surprise.

List words that mean the same as *splendid*.

_____

_____

unique

The armadillo's bony armor makes it a **unique** animal.

What is something that makes you unique?

_____

_____

watchful

The ducklings learned to swim under the **watchful** eyes of their mother.

When do you need to be watchful?

_____

_____

Synonyms

Synonyms are words that have the same meaning. Use them as context clues to figure out the meaning of words you don't know.

FIND TEXT EVIDENCE

On page 43, I'm not sure what tricky *means. I see the context clue* clever *in the same sentence. I know that* clever *means "smart and skillful." I think* tricky *and* clever *are synonyms. They have almost the same meaning. Now I know that* tricky *means "smart and skillful."*

Turtle was angry that Anansi had tricked him. But he was also tricky and clever.

Your Turn Find a synonym for this word from the folktale.

awkward, page 44 _____

_____

CHECK IN ▶ 1 ▶ 2 ▶ 3 ▶ 4 ▶

Visualize

Authors use colorful words and details to help readers visualize, or form pictures, in their minds. This helps readers understand the actions and feelings of characters in a story.

🔍 **FIND TEXT EVIDENCE**

Reread page 42 of "Anansi Learns a Lesson." You might not be sure why Turtle feels upset. Use the details in this part of the story to visualize how he feels.

Page 42

Turtle was upset and filled with **dismay**. He knew his hands were clean, but he went to wash them again. When he returned Anansi had eaten all of the fruit.

I read that Turtle is upset and filled with dismay when he has to wash his hands again. He knows they are already clean. These details help me figure out that Turtle feels confused and frustrated about having to wash his hands a second time.

Your Turn Reread the last two paragraphs on page 44 and the first paragraph on page 45. How do Fish and Turtle trick Anansi? Visualize what happens. Then write the answer here.

_____

_____

CHECK IN ⟩1⟩ 2 ⟩ 3 ⟩ 4

Theme

"Anansi Learns a Lesson" is a **folktale**. A folktale

- is a short story passed from parents to children in a culture
- has a theme, or message, that the author wants the reader to learn from the story

🔍 FIND TEXT EVIDENCE

I can tell that "Anansi Learns a Lesson" is a folktale. It's a short story with a theme that develops throughout the plot.

Page 45

"Welcome, Anansi," said Turtle. "Drop those stones and help yourself."

As soon as Anansi dropped the stones, he rocketed to the surface of the lake. Anansi sputtered furiously. "Fish and Turtle tricked me," he cried angrily.

Back at the bottom of the lake, Turtle and Fish laughed and laughed.

"Anansi has tricked us many times," said Turtle. "For once, we tricked him."

Summarize

Look at your notes and think about what happens in "Anansi Learns a Lesson." Use the theme and plot events to summarize the text.

Readers to Writers

Think about the lesson in "Anansi Learns a Lesson." When you write, think about using what characters do and feel to help your readers understand the theme of your story.

Theme

Authors use details, such as plot events and the actions of characters, to develop the theme. A lesson that a character learns at the end of a story can help readers understand the story's theme.

Your Turn Think about the lesson that Anansi learns in "Anansi Learns a Lesson." What is the theme, or message, that the author wants readers to understand?

COLLABORATE

_____

_____

_____

CHECK IN ▶ 1 〉 2 〉 3 〉 4

Character Perspective

A character's perspective is the character's attitude, or feelings, toward someone or something. Characters in a story often have different perspectives. To understand a character's perspective, look for details that reveal the character's thoughts and actions.

 FIND TEXT EVIDENCE

I can look for details on page 42 that show what Anansi says and what he does. These details can help me understand his perspective toward sharing his lunch with Turtle.

Details
Anansi eats half the bananas while Turtle washes his hands.
Anansi finishes the bananas while Turtle washes his hands a second time.
Anansi says, "Ha, ha, I tricked you, Turtle."

↓

Perspective
Anansi does not want to share his lunch and thinks tricking Turtle is funny.

 Your Turn Reread page 45 of "Anansi Learns a Lesson." Find details that show Turtle's perspective toward Anansi. Write the details and Turtle's perspective in the graphic organizer.

Quick Tip

Perspective is not the same as point of view. Point of view refers to who is telling the story. "Anansi Learns a Lesson" is told in the third-person point of view. This means the narrator is not a character in the story.

CHECK IN 1 ⟩ 2 ⟩ 3 ⟩ 4

Details

Perspective

I can use text evidence to respond to a folktale.

Respond to Reading

COLLABORATE

Talk about the prompt below. Use your notes and evidence from the text to support your answer.

Why is "Anansi Learns a Lesson" a good title for this folktale?

_____

_____

_____

_____

_____

_____

_____

_____

_____

_____

Quick Tip

Use these sentence starters to talk about the folktale.

Anansi tricks Turtle by . . .

I read that . . .

This is a good title because . . .

Grammar Connections

Pay attention to verb tenses. "Anansi Learns a Lesson" uses the past tense. But since the events in it never really happened, your response should use the present tense. For example, instead of writing "Anansi tricked Turtle," write, "Anansi tricks Turtle."

CHECK IN 1 > 2 > 3 > 4 >

Animal Life Cycles

COLLABORATE

Different kinds of animals have unique life cycles, or changes they experience throughout their lives. Work with a partner to research an animal of your choice. Then draw a diagram of its life cycle.

Step 1 **Set a Goal** Choose an animal to research.

Step 2 **Identify Sources** Use key words in an online search engine to find reliable websites with information on the life cycle of your animal.

Step 3 **Find and Record Information** Take notes and cite your sources. Find information that tells if your animal is a mammal, bird, reptile, amphibian, fish, or something else. How does the way your animal looks change throughout its life?

Step 4 **Organize and Combine Information** Organize your notes by sorting information into each stage of your animal's life cycle.

Step 5 **Create and Present** Create your diagram. Use the diagram of a frog's life cycle as a model. Think of how you will present your diagram to the class.

> **Quick Tip**
>
> Key words are words or phrases related to your topic. We use key words to find results in online searches. If your key words are too general, you'll get too many results. Use specific key words to find the information you need.

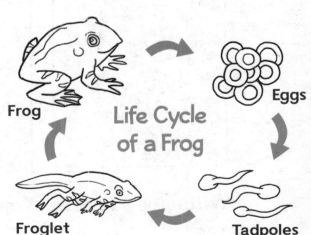
Frog
Eggs
Life Cycle of a Frog
Froglet
Tadpoles

CHECK IN ▶ 1 ⟩ 2 ⟩ 3 ⟩ 4

Martina the Beautiful Cockroach

? How does the author help you visualize how Martina feels about Don Cerdo, the pig?

COLLABORATE

Talk About It Reread **Literature Anthology** page 223. Talk with a partner about how Don Cerdo smells and what Martina does.

Cite Text Evidence What clues help you understand how quickly Martina wants to get rid of Don Cerdo? Write text evidence and explain what it helps you visualize and understand.

Literature Anthology: pages 212–231

Evaluate Information

Notice the author's use of punctuation. How do exclamation points help you visualize how Don Cerdo smells?

Don Cerdo	What Martina Does	I Visualize

Write The author helps me visualize how Martina feels about Don

Cerdo by _____

_____

CHECK IN 1 2 3 4

How do you know what kind of character Don Lagarto is?

Talk About It Reread **Literature Anthology** page 225. Talk to a partner about how the author describes Don Lagarto, the lizard.

Cite Text Evidence What clues help you get to know what the lizard is like? Write text evidence in the chart.

Clues	What It Means

Write I know what kind of character Don Lagarto is because

the author _____

_____

_____

Quick Tip

Use these sentence starters to talk about Don Lagarto, the lizard.

The author describes the lizard . . .

This makes me think he is . . .

 Synthesize Information

Make connections between what happens earlier in the story and Martina's meeting with Don Lagarto. Talk about what kind of mood you think Martina is in when Don Lagarto shows up.

CHECK IN 1 2 3 4

? **How does the author help you understand how the little mouse and Martina are perfect for each other?**

Make Inferences

COLLABORATE

Talk About It Reread **Literature Anthology** pages 230 and 231. Discuss how the mouse is different from the other suitors.

Cite Text Evidence What qualities does the little mouse have that make him perfect for Martina? Write them in the chart.

An inference is a conclusion based on facts. Use text evidence about the little mouse and Martina to infer why they make a perfect match.

Quality	Quality	Quality

↓ ↓ ↓

Why the Little Mouse Is Perfect for Martina

Write The author helps me understand that the little mouse is

perfect for Martina by _____

_____

_____

CHECK IN ▶ 1 ⟩ 2 ⟩ 3 ⟩ 4 ⟩

Respond to Reading

COLLABORATE

Talk about the prompt below. Use your notes and evidence from the text to support your answer.

Why might it be tricky for Martina to pick the right husband?

_____

_____

_____

_____

_____

_____

_____

_____

_____

_____

Quick Tip

Use these sentence starters to talk about the prompt.

It's tricky for Martina to pick the right husband because . . .

Martina's suitors are . . .

This helps me understand . . .

CHECK IN 1 2 3 4

Get a Backbone!

Literature Anthology:
pages 234–237

1   Most animals in the world fit in one of two groups. Some have backbones. The others do not. People, lizards, owls, frogs, and sharks all have backbones. Touch the back of your neck. That's where your backbone starts. It's a string of bones that goes all the way down your back to your tailbone.

2   What would you be like without a backbone? You couldn't walk or sit up. You'd have to slither around like a worm or swim like an octopus. Those animals have no backbones.

3   Animals with backbones are called vertebrates. All vertebrates have backbones. However, not all vertebrates are alike. They have different features. Some are tiny. Others are huge. Some swim, while others fly.

4   Vertebrates can be birds, amphibians, fish, reptiles, or mammals. Animals in each group share a unique quality that makes them special.

Reread and use the prompts to take notes in the text.

In paragraph 1, **draw a box around** how the author helps you understand what a backbone is. Then look at the photograph. How does it help you understand more about the backbone?

_____

_____

_____

Reread paragraph 2. **Circle** words that help you visualize how animals without backbones move.

COLLABORATE

Reread paragraphs 3 and 4. With a partner, **underline** words and phrases the author uses to help you visualize different kinds of vertebrates.

Birds

5   Most birds can fly, but bees and bats can, too! Some birds, like ostriches and penguins, can't fly at all. Ostriches run. Penguins walk and swim. So what makes birds special?

6   Feathers, of course! Feathers keep birds warm. They can help birds to fly and steer through the air. The color of a bird's feathers can help it hide from predators or attract other birds.

Reptiles

7   Lizards and snakes are reptiles. All reptiles have scales covering their bodies.

8   Because reptiles are cold-blooded, they must live in warm places. Some snakes, turtles, and crocodiles live mostly in warm water. Some reptiles live in dry deserts. Most reptiles have low bodies, four short legs, and a tail. Only snakes have no legs at all.

Reread paragraphs 5 and 6. **Write a number before** each sentence that says how birds can be different from each other. Then **circle** the sentence that states what all birds have in common.

COLLABORATE

Reread paragraph 8. Talk with a partner about what *cold-blooded* means. **Underline** how the author helps you understand what that means.

Then **draw a box around** two places where reptiles live. Write them here:

1 _____

2 _____

? **How does the author organize information to help you understand vertebrates?**

Talk About It Reread the excerpt on page 58. Talk with a partner about what the author does to make information about vertebrates easier to understand.

Cite Text Evidence How does the author organize information? Write evidence in the chart.

Reread the excerpt on page 58.

> **Quick Tip**
>
> As you reread each paragraph, look for sentences that help you understand or visualize its central idea.

Text Evidence	How It Helps

Write The author helps me understand vertebrates by

_____

_____

CHECK IN 1 2 3 4

Compare and Contrast

Authors use text structure to make their writing easier to understand. A common form of text structure in informational writing is compare and contrast. This is when an author shows how two things are alike and different.

 FIND TEXT EVIDENCE

On page 59 of "Get a Backbone!" the author uses compare and contrast to help you understand why birds are unique.

> Most birds can fly, but bees and bats can, too! Some birds, like ostriches and penguins, can't fly at all. Ostriches run. Penguins walk and swim. So what makes birds special?
>
> Feathers, of course!

Your Turn Reread the last two paragraphs on page 59.

- How does the author help you understand more about reptiles?

_____

_____

- What is something all reptiles share? _____

_____

Readers to Writers

Showing how two things are alike and different is a great way to help your reader understand a topic. Signal words and phrases, such as *alike, also, both, unlike,* and *instead of,* can help you compare and contrast.

CHECK IN 1 2 3 4

? How is the way George Stubbs painted a zebra like the ways the authors of *Martina the Beautiful Cockroach* and "Get a Backbone!" describe different animals?

Talk About It Look at the painting and read the caption. Talk with a partner about what makes this animal unique.

Cite Text Evidence **Underline** text evidence in the caption that tells how the zebra is unique. **Circle** two clues in the painting that show you. Think about how the authors of *Martina the Beautiful Cockroach* and "Get a Backbone!" use words and phrases to do the same.

Write Both the artist and the authors

describe animals by _____

_____

_____

_____

_____

_____

_____

> **Quick Tip**
>
> I can use details in the painting to help me compare it to what I have read.

English artist George Stubbs painted "Zebra" in 1763. It's a painting of the first zebra to be seen in England. Stubbs made sure his painting looked exactly like the live animal by painting the zebra's ears facing backward and copying the stripes perfectly.

CHECK IN ❯ 1 ❯ 2 ❯ 3 ❯ 4 ❯

My Goal I know what makes different animals unique.

Write an Animal Tale

Review what you learned about what makes different animals unique. How do unique traits help solve problems? Use what you learned from the texts to write an animal tale of your own.

1 Look at your Build Knowledge notes in your reader's notebook.

2 Write a short animal tale using at least three of the animal characters you read about. You can also add characters of your own. Your characters should use their unique traits to solve a problem. Use new vocabulary words in your tale.

3 Create an illustrated cover to go with your story. Share your tale with the class.

Think about what you learned in this text set. Fill in the bars on page 39.

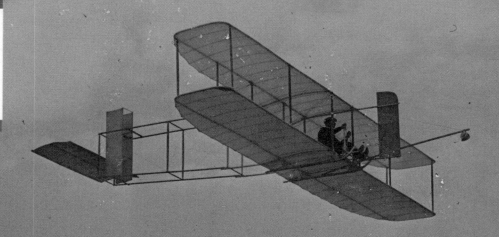

The Wright brothers tested their glider many times.
Their experiments were important.

Build Vocabulary

Write new words you learned about the past. Draw lines and circles for the words you write.

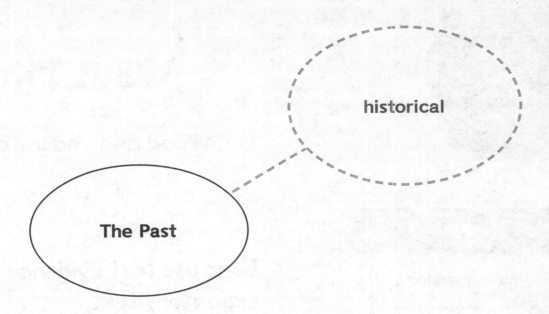

historical

The Past

Go online to **my.mheducation.com** and read the Blast titled "The Caddo." Think about why learning about events and people from history is important. Then blast back your response.

Think about what you already know. Fill in the bars. Let's keep learning!

What I Know Now

I can read and understand expository text.

1 > 2 > 3 > 4

I can use text evidence to respond to expository text.

1 > 2 > 3 > 4

I know what makes historical events unique.

1 > 2 > 3 > 4

Key

1 = I do not understand.

2 = I understand but need more practice.

3 = I understand.

4 = I understand and can teach someone.

STOP You will come back to the next page later.

Think about what you learned. Fill in the bars. Keep working hard!

What I Learned

I can read and understand expository text.

1 > 2 > 3 > 4

I can use text evidence to respond to expository text.

1 > 2 > 3 > 4

I know what makes historical events unique.

1 > 2 > 3 > 4

My Goal I can read and understand expository text.

TAKE NOTES

As you read, make note of interesting words and important information.

TIME for KiDS

Moving America FORWARD

Essential Question

?

How is each event in history unique?

Read to see how the Model T changed the way people move.

Model T cars were strong and reliable. Many people in America drove them.

Henry Ford introduced the Ford Model T car in 1908. The original **vehicles** came in blue, gray, green, and red. They cost $850 to buy. Everyone wanted a Model T, and thanks to the moving assembly line, almost everyone could have one. By 1918, half of all cars in the United States were Model Ts.

Everybody Wants One

The Model T was not the first car ever made, but it was the one most people could afford to buy at the time. One of the **resources** Ford used to build the Model T was steel. The car, which was nicknamed "Tin Lizzie," was built to hold up on rough roads. It was dependable and easy to drive. They were also simple to maintain, or fix. As the nation's **population** grew, more and more people were buying cars. They wanted to own a Model T.

Before the Model T, cars were expensive. Not everyone had enough money to own one. Ford knew that he needed to bring the price down. First he found a way to make more cars to meet the demand. Then he built them faster. Finally, he was able to make them affordable, or lower the cost so more people could buy one.

The first Model T hit the roads on October 1, 1908. It could travel at a speed of 45 miles per hour.

EXPOSITORY TEXT

FIND TEXT EVIDENCE

Read

Paragraph 1

Summarize

Underline details about the Ford Model T car. Summarize the text in your own words.

Paragraph 2

Suffixes

Draw a box around the word *dependable*. Write what *dependable* means.

Paragraph 3

Chronology

Circle actions Ford took to lower the price of the Model T car.

Reread

Author's Craft

Reread the second paragraph. How does the author help you understand what *maintain* means?

TIME for KiDS

Paragraph 1

Summarize

Underline how Ford improved the assembly line. Then summarize in your own words.

_____

_____

Paragraphs 2–3

Chronology

Circle what happened after gas tanks and engines were added.

Captions

Look at the photo and caption at the top of the page. What new information do you learn?

_____

_____

How does the author help you understand how an assembly line works?

Assembly Required

Henry Ford did not invent the assembly line. But in 1913, he improved on it. Ford rolled out a moving assembly line that made building cars much faster. One Model T used to take more than 12 hours to build. Using a moving assembly line, workers could build a car in one hour and 33 minutes.

These workers on an assembly line are putting together Model T cars in Detroit, Michigan, in 1927.

To build a Model T, workers and machines worked together. There were 84 steps. First, some workers stood at assembly stations putting small car parts together. Then, a moving conveyer belt carried the car parts along as more workers put them together. After that, the body of the car was pulled along as more workers put their parts onto it. Then the engines and gas tanks were added. Finally, the car bodies were assembled, and the car was finished.

The moving assembly line changed **transportation** in the United States. Workers could build many cars at once. Business **boomed**.

Many inventions have made it safer for people to drive cars.

Timeline: Drive Safely

1880	1890	1900	1910

1885
The first seatbelts were used.

1903
Mary Anderson invented the windshield wiper.

A World on Wheels

The price of the Model T dropped to less than $300 in 1925. More and more people bought them. As a result, more roads and highways were paved. Then gas stations and hotels sprung up. Next, many people moved out of cities. The people who lived in the 1920s started to **appreciate** being able to drive to work or go on a journey. Driving around was an **agreeable** way for them to spend time. Their **descendants** today may find life before cars hard to imagine.

Mary Anderson and the Windshield Wiper

Mary Anderson invented the windshield wiper while riding a streetcar in 1902 during a snowstorm in New York City.

After watching her streetcar driver jump in and out of the streetcar to clear off his icy windshield, Mary had an idea. First, she sketched her idea. Next, she worked out a plan. Then, Mary built a model out of rubber, wood, and metal. Finally, in 1903, she tested it. It worked!

By 1913, more people bought cars. Thanks to Mary Anderson, they had windshield wipers.

Summarize

Review your notes. Use the text's central idea and relevant details to summarize "Moving America Forward."

1920   1930   1940

1915
Cars stopped at the first stop sign.

1938
Cars first used turn signals.

(tl)Popperfoto/Getty Images, (tb)Richard Allen/Flair Talent/Image Source, (tbc)Image Source/Getty Images, (br)Bettmann/Getty Images

FIND TEXT EVIDENCE

Read

Paragraph 1

Chronology

What happened after gas stations and hotels sprung up?

_____

_____

_____

Underline the signal word.

Timelines

What happened in 1915?

_____

_____

_____

Circle the year cars first used turn signals.

Reread

Author's Craft

Why is "A World on Wheels" a good heading for this section?

Vocabulary

Use the sentences to talk with a partner about each word. Then answer the questions.

agreeable

Eric loves warm weather that is pleasant and **agreeable**.

What kind of weather do you find agreeable?

_____

_____

appreciate

Jan and Kayla **appreciate** everything their grandmother does for them.

How do you show people that you appreciate them?

_____

_____

Build Your Word List Pick an interesting word you listed on page 68. Use a print or online dictionary to find the word's meaning. In your reader's notebook, make a list of words with almost the same meaning.

boomed

Juan's lemonade business **boomed** in the summer, and he sold more lemonade than ever before.

Boomed has multiple meanings. Can you name another word with multiple meanings?

_____

_____

descendants

Ann and her family are **descendants** of the people in the photographs.

What are descendants?

_____

_____

population

There is a large **population** of flamingos living in the pond.

Name another animal population that might live in a pond.

_____

_____

resources

Plants need **resources**, such as sunlight and fresh air, to grow.

What resources do people need?

_____

_____

transportation

Trains are a favorite form of **transportation** for many people.

Write a sentence about your favorite form of transportation.

_____

_____

vehicles

Vehicles are parked in a parking lot.

What type of vehicle do you travel to school in?

_____

_____

Suffixes

A suffix is a word part that is added to the end of a word. It changes the word's meaning. The suffix *-able* means "is able or can be."

🔍 **FIND TEXT EVIDENCE**

I see the word reliable *in the caption on page 68.* Reliable *has the base word* rely*. I know that* rely *means "to trust or depend." The suffix* -able *means "is able or can be." I think the word* reliable *means "able to be trusted."*

Model T cars were strong and reliable.

Your Turn Use the suffix to figure out the meaning of the word.

affordable, page 69 _____

_____

CHECK IN　1〉2〉3〉4〉

Summarize

When you summarize, you retell the central idea and relevant details in a text. Use the details in "Moving America Forward" to help you summarize the text.

FIND TEXT EVIDENCE

Why did many people want to buy the Model T car? Reread "Everybody Wants One" on page 69. Evaluate and decide which details are most important. Then use the key ideas to summarize the text in your own words.

> ### Quick Tip
> When you evaluate details, you look for words and phrases that help you identify the most important ideas in the text. Then use the key ideas to summarize the text in your own words.

Page 69

Everybody Wants One

The Model T was not the first car ever made, but it was the one most people could afford to buy at the time. One of the **resources** Ford used to build the Model T was steel. The car, which was nicknamed "Tin Lizzie," was built to hold up on rough roads. It was dependable and easy to drive. They were also simple to maintain, or fix. As the nation's **population** grew, more and more people were buying cars. They wanted to own a Model T.

I read that the Model T was the car *most people could afford to buy.* *The Model T was dependable and easy to drive. It was also simple to maintain, or fix. These details are important. They help me summarize. Many people wanted to buy the Model T because it didn't cost too much and it was easy to drive and take care of.*

 Your Turn Reread "Assembly Required" on page 70. Use the central idea and relevant details to summarize the text.

_____

_____

CHECK IN ⟩ 1 ⟩ 2 ⟩ 3 ⟩ 4 ⟩

Timelines and Captions

"Moving America Forward" is an **expository text**. An expository text

- has the purpose of informing the reader about a topic
- has text features, such as timelines, photographs, and captions

🔍 **FIND TEXT EVIDENCE**

I can tell "Moving America Forward" is an expository text. The author's purpose is to inform the reader about Ford and the Model T. There are text features that add meaning to the text.

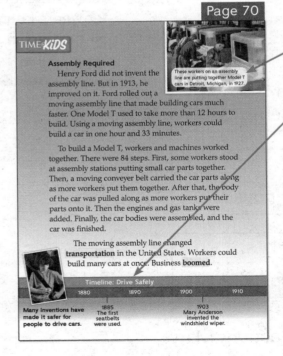

Page 70

Captions
Photographs and captions give additional facts and details.

Timelines
A timeline shows the chronology, or time order, of important dates and events.

Your Turn Review the timeline on pages 70 and 71. What is something you learned? How does the timeline add meaning to "Moving America Forward"?

_____

_____

_____

CHECK IN 〉 1 〉 2 〉 3 〉 4

Chronology

Chronology is the order in which important events take place. Look for words and phrases that show time order, such as *first, next, then, later that day, after that,* and *finally*. These signal words show the order of events.

 FIND TEXT EVIDENCE

In the section titled "A World on Wheels" on page 71, the author describes in time order how the world changed as more and more cars became available. Signal words and phrases, such as next *and* as a result, *show the order of events.*

Quick Tip

Authors can also use dates to show chronology, or time order. In the first paragraph on page 69, the year 1908 tells when Henry Ford first introduced the Model T car. Later in the paragraph, the year 1918 shows that ten years later, half of all the cars in the U.S. were Model T cars.

Event

The price of the Model T dropped to less than $300 in 1925. More and more people bought them.

↓

Event

As a result, more roads and highways were paved.

↓

Event

Then gas stations and hotels sprung up.

COLLABORATE

Your Turn Reread the sidebar on page 71. List the actions Mary Anderson took to invent the windshield wiper. Write the events in order in your graphic organizer. Use signal words.

CHECK IN ⟩ 1 ⟩ 2 ⟩ 3 ⟩ 4 ⟩

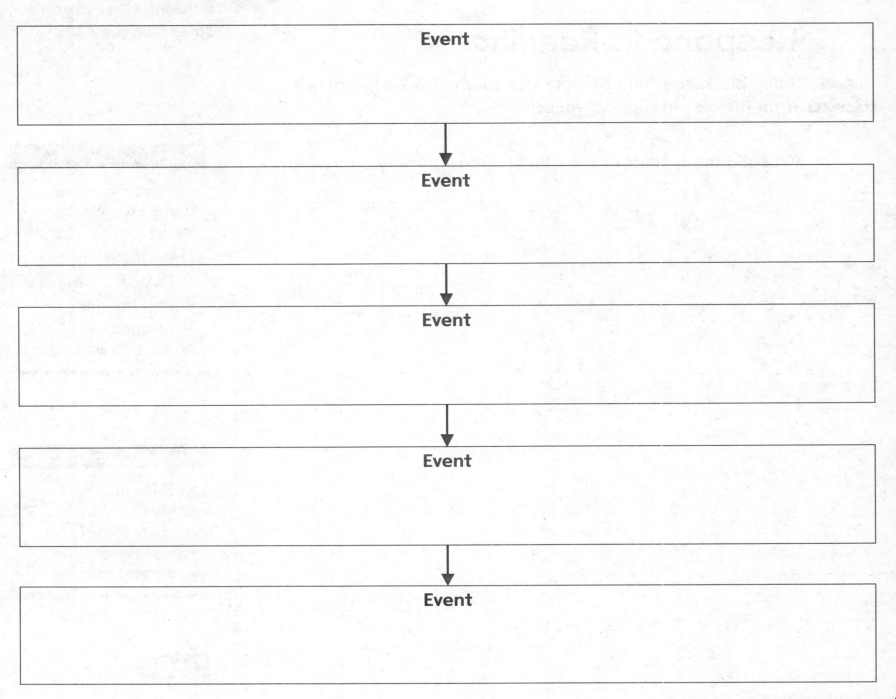

Event

Event

Event

Event

Event

Respond to Reading

Talk about the prompt below. Use your notes and evidence from the text to support your answer.

Why did the success of the Model T move America forward?

_____

_____

_____

_____

_____

_____

_____

_____

_____

_____

_____

_____

Quick Tip

Use these sentence starters to talk about the prompt.

I read that . . .

The Model T car was a success because . . .

This helped move America forward by . . .

Grammar Connections

As you write your response, try to combine some of your sentences using interesting verbs.

CHECK IN ⟩ 1 ⟩ 2 ⟩ 3 ⟩ 4 ⟩

Important Events in History

Authors write about unique historical events in news articles in newspapers, magazines, and websites. Work with a partner to research an important or memorable event from the past. Then write your own news article about it.

Step 1 **Set a Goal** Choose a historical event to research.

Step 2 **Identify Sources** Use the library or internet to find primary and secondary sources related to your topic.

Step 3 **Find and Record Information** Gather information about your topic by analyzing your sources. Why is the event you chose unique or memorable? What happened? When did it happen? Who was involved?

Step 4 **Organize and Combine Information** Organize your notes. Decide which details you want to include in your article. Start to think about a headline you might use.

Step 5 **Create and Present** Write your article and final headline. Choose photos or draw illustrations to go with what you wrote.

The World News

ASTRONAUTS WALK ON THE MOON

"One Small Step for a Man, One Giant Leap for Mankind"

(newspaper)Rangizzz/123RF, (photo)NASA Headquarters - GReatest Images of NASA (NASA-HQ-GRIN)

CHECK IN ⟩ 1 ⟩ 2 ⟩ 3 ⟩ 4 ⟩

Birth of an Anthem

Literature Anthology: pages 238–241

? How does the way the author organizes the text help you understand how America's national anthem was created?

 Talk About It Reread **Literature Anthology** pages 240 and 241. Talk with a partner about what inspired Francis Scott Key to write "The Star-Spangled Banner."

Cite Text Evidence What clues does the author use to help you understand the cause-and-effect structure of the text? Write text evidence in the chart.

 **Make Inferences**

Use text evidence and what you know to make an inference. An inference is a conclusion based on facts. What inference can you make about why "The Star-Spangled Banner" became one of America's most beloved songs?

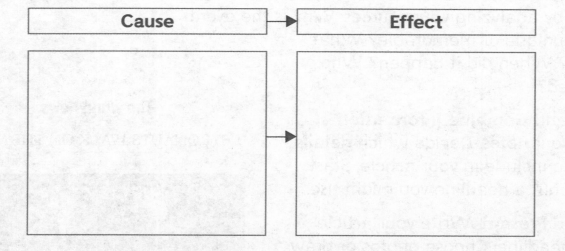

Cause	→	Effect

Write The author organizes the text to help me understand _____

_____

_____

CHECK IN ⟩ 1 ⟩ 2 ⟩ 3 ⟩ 4 ⟩

How does the sidebar help you understand where America's patriotic anthems come from?

 Talk About It Reread the sidebar on **Literature Anthology** page 240. Talk with a partner about how the sidebar helps you understand what unofficial anthems are.

Cite Text Evidence Sidebars contribute, or add, meaning to a text by giving new information. How is the information in the sidebar different from that in the selection? Write examples.

Quick Tip

Use these sentence starters to talk about the sidebar.

The information in the sidebar is about . . .

The author includes the sidebar to help me understand . . .

Birth of an Anthem	Sidebar

Write The author uses the sidebar to help me understand that

_____

_____

_____

CHECK IN 1 2 3 4

Respond to Reading

COLLABORATE Talk about the prompt below. Use your notes and evidence from the text to support your answer.

Why do you think "The Star-Spangled Banner" became the national anthem?

_____

_____

_____

_____

_____

_____

_____

_____

_____

_____

_____

_____

Quick Tip

Use these sentence starters to talk about the prompt.

Francis Scott Key was inspired by . . .

"The Star-Spangled Banner" is the national anthem because . . .

CHECK IN 1 > 2 > 3 > 4

Discovering Life Long Ago

Literature Anthology:
pages 242–243

[1]   In the past, people wrote in diaries and journals. They wrote letters to friends and families. They also wrote autobiographies to tell their life stories. Diaries, journals, and autobiographies tell us what people thought and felt. They also give details about daily life in the past. They describe the food people ate. They tell what kind of transportation they used.

[2]   Posters, newspapers, and old photographs also give details about events in the past. So do speeches and songs. Photographs show people's clothes and how they had fun.

[3]   Both words and pictures from the past help us see how people lived long ago. They tell a history of people, places, and things. They take us back in time.

Reread and use the prompts to take notes in the text.

Reread paragraphs 1 and 2. **Underline** the ways people used to tell about the way life was long ago. **Number** the sentences that tell different things we can learn. List three of those things here:

1 _____

2 _____

3 _____

COLLABORATE

Talk with a partner about how the author organized the information in this selection. **Circle** the paragraph that summarizes all the information.

How does the author help you understand how people learn about events in the past?

 Talk About It Reread paragraphs 1 and 2 on page 83. Talk with a partner about the ways people learn more about the past.

Cite Text Evidence How does the author arrange the information to help you understand how we learn about life long ago? Write text evidence here.

Quick Tip
When I reread, I can use the way the author shares information to help me understand the topic better.

Paragraph 1	Paragraph 2	This Helps Because ...

Write The author helps me understand how people learn about

the past by _____

_____

_____

_____

CHECK IN 1 2 3 4

Author's Purpose

An author's purpose is the author's reason for writing. In an expository text, the author's purpose is to inform the reader about a topic. Authors can support this purpose by describing the topic in their own words. They can also include primary sources from people with firsthand experience with a topic.

 FIND TEXT EVIDENCE

On page 83 of "Discovering Life Long Ago," the author informs the reader about the past by describing the ways in which people shared their experiences.

> In the past, people wrote in diaries and journals. They wrote letters to friends and families. They also wrote autobiographies to tell their life stories.

 Your Turn Reread Sallie Hester's diary entry on page 243 of "Discovering Life Long Ago" in the **Literature Anthology**.

- How does the selection help you understand the way people lived long ago? _____

_____

Readers to Writers

A diary is an example of a primary source. Information from primary sources helps readers understand what it was like to actually experience an event in the past.

CHECK IN 1 2 3 4

MAKE CONNECTIONS

? **How do the song lyrics help you visualize an event in history in the same way the words and phrases in "Birth of an Anthem" and "Discovering Life Long Ago" do?**

Talk About It Read the song lyrics. Talk with a partner about what Betsy and her brother did.

Cite Text Evidence Circle words and phrases in the song lyrics that tell who went on the journey and what creatures they brought with them. **Underline** clues that show what they did.

Write The song lyrics help me visualize the

journey by _____

_____

_____

_____

_____

_____

from Sweet Betsy from Pike

Oh, do you remember sweet
  Betsy from Pike,
Who crossed the wide prairies
  with her brother Ike?
With two yoke of oxen, a
  big yaller dog,
A tall Shanghai rooster and
  one spotted hog. . . .

They camped on the prairie for
  weeks upon weeks.
They swam the wide rivers and
  crossed the tall peaks.
And soon they were rollin' in
  nuggets of gold.
You may not believe it but
  that's what we're told.

American Folk Song
Adapted by Merrill Staton

CHECK IN 〉 1 〉 2 〉 3 〉 4 〉

I know what makes historical events unique.

Create a Timeline

What did you learn from the texts you read about events in history? Use your knowledge to create a timeline of unique historical events. Use text evidence to explain why it's important to learn about unique events in history.

1 Look at your Build Knowledge notes in your reader's notebook.

2 Select three or more historical events that you read about. Set the events in time order on a timeline. The oldest event should be on the far left of your timeline. The most recent event should be on the right.

3 Beneath each event, add a short description of what happened and why the event is important.

4 Beneath your timeline, write a few sentences that tell why people should learn about events in history. Use new vocabulary words you have learned.

Think about what you learned in this text set. Fill in the bars on page 67.

Think about what you already know. Fill in the bars. It's important to keep learning.

What I Know Now

Key

1 = I do not understand.

2 = I understand but need more practice.

3 = I understand.

4 = I understand and can teach someone.

I can write an opinion essay.

| 1 | 2 | 3 | 4 |

I can synthesize information from three sources.

| 1 | 2 | 3 | 4 |

STOP You will come back to the next page later.

Think about what you learned.
Fill in the bars. What helped you do
your best?

What I Learned

I can write an opinion essay.

1 2 3 4

I can synthesize information from
three sources.

1 2 3 4

WRITE TO SOURCES

You will answer an opinion writing prompt using sources and a rubric.

ANALYZE THE RUBRIC

A rubric tells you what needs to be included in your writing.

Purpose, Focus, and Organization

Read the second bullet. What is an opinion?

An opinion is _____

_____

Evidence and Elaboration

Read the first bullet. **Circle** how to support an opinion.

Read the third bullet. **Underline** and list three ways to elaborate on or support an opinion.

_____

Opinion Writing Rubric

Purpose, Focus, and Organization • Score 4

- Stays focused on the purpose, audience, and task
- States the opinion in a clear way
- Uses transitional strategies, such as the use of signal, or linking, words and phrases, to show how ideas are connected
- Has a logical progression of ideas
- **Begins with a strong introduction and ends with a conclusion**

Evidence and Elaboration • Score 4

- Supports the opinion with convincing details
- Has strong examples of relevant evidence, or supporting details, with references to multiple sources
- Uses elaborative techniques, such as examples, definitions, and quotations from sources
- Uses precise language to express ideas clearly
- Uses appropriate academic and domain-specific language that matches the audience and purpose of the essay
- Uses different sentence types and lengths

Turn to page 244 for the complete Opinion Writing Rubric.

Valentain Jevee/Shutterstock

Opinion

Stating the Opinion A strong opinion essay has a clearly stated opinion. Read the paragraph below. The opinion is highlighted.

> Private companies are working to get tourists into space. NASA is a United States agency that is in charge of space missions. But NASA isn't interested in space tourism. NASA's goal is research. Its job is to learn about space. The FBI is another agency. Private space companies can focus on bringing people into space, so they should control space travel.

What does the opinion tell you about the focus of the essay?

_____

_____

_____

Supporting Details Writers use supporting details as evidence to support their opinions. Strong writers do not include unimportant details in their writing.

Reread the paragraph above. Cross out an unimportant detail that does not support the opinion.

Purpose

Writers have a purpose in mind when they write. They make choices about what to include based on their purpose. Reread the paragraph about space flight. What is the purpose of the essay?

ANALYZE THE STUDENT MODEL

Paragraph 1

Write a detail from Mariana's introduction that caught your attention.

_____

_____

_____

Reread the first paragraph of Mariana's essay. The opinion is highlighted.

Paragraph 2

What is an example of relevant evidence that Mariana uses to support her claim?

_____

_____

_____

Circle the sentence that tells why private space travel is now possible.

Student Model: Opinion Essay

Mariana responded to the writing prompt: *Write an opinion essay about who should control space travel.* Read Mariana's essay below.

1   Have you ever dreamed of walking on the Moon or moving to Mars? Do you wish you could take a wild ride into outer space? Well, your dreams of becoming a space tourist may soon come true. Private companies are working to get tourists into space. NASA is a United States agency that is in charge of space missions. But NASA isn't interested in space tourism. NASA's goal is research. Its job is to learn about space. Private space companies can focus on bringing people into space, so they should control space travel.

2   Private space travel was made legal in 2004. Since then, many companies have entered the space race. One reason private companies should control space travel is because they can compete against each other. This helps them push each other to try new ways of doing things. For instance, NASA hasn't built a reusable rocket. Private companies have. The government can use the new inventions that come from private companies.

3   Private space companies should also control space travel because they can keep down the cost of space tourism. Something like this happened with airplanes in the 1920s. Many years ago, it was mostly the government that used planes. Then, private companies built planes to deliver the mail. The companies realized they could charge tourists to fly on the planes. Soon, many people wanted to fly on planes. Because flying became more common and the companies had to compete with each other, the price of flying went down.

4   If private companies control space travel, they can help NASA focus on research. Private companies won't research like NASA. They can earn money by carrying supplies and astronauts to the International Space Station. They might mine rare metals, such as gold, from asteroids. As a result, NASA can avoid spending time and money on those things.

5   It's a good idea for NASA to leave space travel to the private space companies. That leaves NASA with lots of money and resources to do other things. NASA can do what it does best. NASA can continue learning more about space, our galaxy, and beyond.

JGI/Getty Images

Paragraph 3
Reread the third paragraph. **Underline** an example of elaboration that Mariana uses. What claim does this elaboration support?

_____

_____

_____

Paragraph 4
What is one signal word or phrase Mariana uses to connect her ideas?

_____

_____

Paragraph 5
Reread the conclusion. **Underline** the idea that Mariana repeats from the first paragraph.

Apply the Rubric

With a partner, use the rubric on page 90 to discuss why Mariana scored a 4 on her essay.

Analyze the Prompt

Writing Prompt

You are preparing for a science debate at school. Write an opinion essay about whether robots or people should explore space.

Purpose, Audience, and Task Reread the writing prompt. What is your purpose for writing? My purpose is to _____

_____

Who will your audience be? My audience will be _____

_____

What type of writing is the prompt asking for? _____

_____

Set a Purpose for Reading Sources Asking questions about which is a better way to explore space will help you figure out your purpose for reading. Before you read the passage set about space exploration, write a question here.

_____

_____

_____

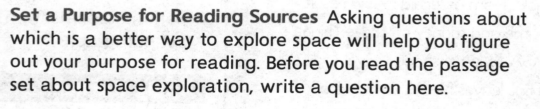

Read the following passage set.

SPACE IS THE PLACE

1   Plans for sending astronauts to Mars will begin in the 2020s. Some say that human space travel is too costly and dangerous. We have robots that can do the job. You don't even have to feed them! **However, humans should explore space because of their many advantages over robots.**

2   One advantage is that people are faster than robots. Rovers are a kind of robot. They have been exploring Mars since 2003. Steve Squyres is a Mars rover scientist. He says, "Most things our rovers can do in a day on Mars, a human explorer could do in less than a minute."

3   A second advantage is human curiosity. Robots can't recognize something unexpected. They may miss an important discovery.

4   People need to explore space for themselves. As president John F. Kennedy said, "We choose to go to the Moon in this decade and do the other things, not because they are easy, but because they are hard." Going to Mars will be very hard, but it is what humans do. We push beyond barriers. We discover new worlds.

Katy Flaty/Shutterstock

OPINION ESSAY

FIND TEXT EVIDENCE 🔍

Paragraph 1
Reread the highlighted opinion in paragraph 1.

Paragraphs 2–3
Underline the two advantages of people exploring space. Write them here.

_____

_____

Paragraph 4
Why is it important for humans to explore space?

_____

_____

_____

_____

Take Notes Summarize the opinion of the source. Give examples that support the opinion.

FIND TEXT EVIDENCE 🔍

Paragraph 5

Reread the highlighted detail in paragraph 5. How does this detail support the opinion?

_____

_____

Paragraph 6

Underline the advantage of sending robots on a space mission.

Paragraphs 7–11

There are risks, or problems, with sending people into space. Write four risks here.

_____

_____

_____

_____

📝 **Take Notes** Summarize the opinion of the source. Give examples that support that opinion.

ROBOTS IN SPACE!

5   Humans who explore space need air, water, and food to survive. Robots do not have these needs. **A lot of time and money goes into making space exploration safe for humans.** Robots should carry out space missions because it would be safer and cheaper.

6   Astronauts must return to Earth after their space mission. Return trips double mission costs and risks. Robots don't have to return to Earth.

7   A mission to Mars would take three years. There would be many risks. One risk is the lack of gravity. The weightlessness of space causes muscles to weaken.

8   Astronauts would live together in a small space for three years. This would be hard for the astronauts' emotional health. Robots don't have bad moods.

9   Another risk is the astronauts' health. They would have little fresh food. Their immune systems would become stressed. Astronauts can become sick.

10   Radioactive rays from the Sun are very dangerous. They may damage robots, but they could cause severe injury to an astronaut.

11   Human space travel is too costly and dangerous. People invented robots to take on the dangerous job of space exploration. We should let them.

A Team That Works!

12   Astronauts and robots must work together to explore space. Astronauts plan on visiting Mars in the next decade. Scientists want to know more about the planet. A robot was sent to Mars to gather information. That information is important to astronauts. After all, they will be the ones who someday explore Mars.

13   The number of people who graduated with science degrees grew from 1961 to 1972. Those are the same years that astronauts went to the Moon. The Moon program inspired students to gain science degrees.

14   Robots are great for exploring outer space, while astronauts are great for inspiring us. A team of robots and astronauts make for the best mission to Mars.

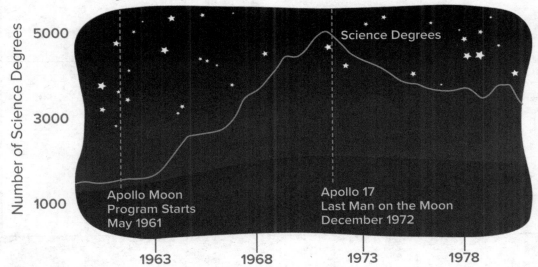

Space Exploration's Impact on Science Degrees

Number of Science Degrees

5000 — Science Degrees

3000

1000 — Apollo Moon Program Starts May 1961 — Apollo 17 Last Man on the Moon December 1972

1963   1968   1973   1978

NASA/JSC Robert Markowitz

FIND TEXT EVIDENCE 🔍

Paragraph 12
Underline the opinion statement in paragraph 12.

Circle the evidence that supports the opinion.

Paragraphs 13–14
Why is human space travel important?

_____

_____

Graph
Look at where the Apollo Moon program begins on the graph. What happened to the number of science degrees after that? Explain why the numbers have changed.

_____

_____

_____

My Goal I can synthesize information from three sources.

TAKE NOTES

Read the writing prompt below. Use the three sources, your notes, and the graphic organizer to plan a response.

Writing Prompt *Write an opinion essay about whether robots or people should explore space.*

Synthesize Information

Review the relevant evidence from each source. How does the evidence support your opinion about space exploration? Discuss your ideas with a partner.

Plan: Organize Ideas

Opinion	Supporting Claims
Robots/people should explore space.	One reason for this is . . .

Valentain Jevee/Shutterstock

Relevant Evidence		
Source 1	Source 2	Source 3

Draft: Introductions

Strong Openings Use a strong opening to introduce your topic. One way is to use questions or fascinating facts to grab the reader's attention. A strong opening states the topic in a way that makes the reader want to keep reading.

Reread the first paragraph of the space flight essay. Talk with a partner about text evidence you can use to answer the question.

Ingram Publishing/SuperStock

> Have you ever dreamed of walking on the Moon or moving to Mars? Do you wish you could take a wild ride into outer space? Well, your dreams of becoming a space tourist may soon come true. Private companies are working to get tourists into space. NASA is a United States agency that is in charge of space missions.

How does the author make you want to keep reading?

_____

_____

_____

Draft Use your graphic organizer and example above to write your draft in your writer's notebook. Before you start writing, review the rubric on page 90. Remember to indent the first line of each paragraph.

Quick Tip

When you write your draft, you can include transition words to connect your ideas in a clear way. Use words and phrases such as *however, next, as a result,* and *finally.*

CHECK IN 1 2 3 4

Revise: Peer Conferences

Review a Draft Listen actively to your partner. Take notes about what you liked and what was difficult to follow. Begin by telling what you liked. Use these sentence starters.

I like the evidence you used to support your opinion because . . .

What did you mean by . . .

I think your opening . . .

After you give each other feedback, reflect on the peer conference. What suggestion was the most helpful?

_____

_____

_____

Revision Use the Revising Checklist to help you figure out what text you may need to move, elaborate on, or delete. After you finish writing your final draft, use the full rubric on pages 244–247 to score your essay.

✓ Revising Checklist

- ☐ Does my writing have a strong opinion?
- ☐ Did I include enough relevant evidence to support my opinion?
- ☐ Do I have a strong introduction?
- ☐ Did I check my spelling and punctuation?

Next, you'll write an opinion essay on a new topic.

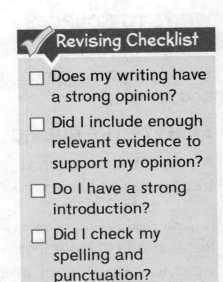

My Score

Purpose, Focus, & Organization (4 pts)	Evidence & Elaboration (4 pts)	Conventions (2 pts)	Total (10 pts)

WRITE TO SOURCES

You will answer an opinion writing prompt using sources and a rubric.

ANALYZE THE RUBRIC

A rubric tells you what needs to be included in your writing.

Purpose, Focus, and Organization

Read the fifth bullet. Write two ways to support your opinion in an essay.

_____

_____

Evidence and Elaboration

Read the second bullet. What is relevant evidence?

Relevant evidence is _____

_____

_____

Read the last three bullets. **Underline** four things you can do to support relevant evidence in your opinion essay.

Opinion Writing Rubric

Purpose, Focus, and Organization • Score 4

- Stays focused on the purpose, audience, and task
- States the opinion in a clear way
- Uses transitional strategies, such as the use of signal, or linking, words and phrases, to show how ideas are connected
- Has a logical progression of ideas
- Begins with a strong introduction and ends with a conclusion

Evidence and Elaboration • Score 4

- Supports the opinion with convincing details
- **Has strong examples of relevant evidence, or supporting details, with references to multiple sources**
- Uses elaborative techniques, such as examples, definitions, and quotations from sources
- Uses precise language to express ideas clearly
- Uses appropriate academic and domain-specific language that matches the audience and purpose of the essay
- Uses different sentence types and lengths

Turn to page 244 for the complete Opinion Writing Rubric.

Relevant Evidence

Use Relevant Evidence In a strong opinion essay, the opinion is supported by evidence from sources. This evidence should be relevant, or directly related to the opinion.

Read the passage below. Underline evidence that supports the opinion: *Trains are the easiest and most comfortable way to travel.*

The Best Way to Go

There's no doubt: Airplanes are the fastest form of travel. However, airplane travelers often spend hours waiting in lines at the airport. This adds hours to a trip. Travelers can skip the lines and frustration by taking the train instead. Railway passengers can usually just board the train with their ticket. Seats are more spacious and comfortable than the average airplane seat.

Reference Sources When you include evidence from a source, you need to reference that source in your essay. This gives credit to the source for providing the information.

Reread the paragraph. Notice the relevant evidence you underlined. Write a sentence that supports the opinion above. Remember to reference the passage.

Audience

Strong writers think about their audience when writing opinion essays. They may focus on certain ideas that the audience would find interesting. Depending on the audience, the writer may use formal or informal language. Reread "The Best Way to Go." Does the writer use formal or informal language? Why would the writer use this type of language for their audience?

_____

_____

ANALYZE THE STUDENT MODEL

Paragraph 1

Circle the opinion of Darren's essay.

Reread the first paragraph. What reasons does Darren give to support his opinion?

_____

_____

_____

Paragraph 2

Read paragraph 2. The claim in the paragraph is highlighted. How does Darren use Florida as an example to elaborate on this claim?

_____

_____

_____

Paragraph 3

Underline relevant evidence from a source that supports the idea that planes are the fastest way to travel over water.

Student Model: Opinion Essay

Darren responded to the prompt: *Write an opinion essay for a children's travel magazine about whether or not airplanes are the best way to travel.* Read Darren's essay below.

1 The first successful airplane flew in 1903. For the first time in history, people could fly! Today, airplanes are a regular part of life. Air travel lets people see the world in a fast and safe way. That's why airplanes are the best way to travel.

2 Why do millions of people fly every day? It may be because it is easy to get almost anywhere by plane. The Department of Transportation's website lists thousands of airports around the world. In fact, there are thirteen international airports in Florida alone! People may complain about airport security and wait times. But security checks are needed to keep passengers safe.

3 Airplanes are the fastest way to travel. In the past, ships were the only way to cross the ocean. The article "From Shore to Shore" states that crossing the Atlantic Ocean by boat took over five weeks. Today, a flight is just eight hours. When traveling over land, some people go by car

or train. A drive or train ride from Washington to Florida takes over two days. But a flight is under five hours. People can get where they're going quickly instead of traveling for days.

4   The safest way to travel is by plane. The article "The Best Way to Go" describes a study by Northwestern University. It compared the number of serious accidents in different vehicles. Airplanes topped the list as the safest vehicle to travel in. That's no surprise! Many safety tests are done on planes before they fly. Pilots get years of training. Planes get even safer as technology improves.

5   Air travel connects people and places. This is the greatest benefit of flying. World leaders can meet face-to-face. Emergency workers can rush to places in need. People can travel to new places and learn about different cultures. These things were difficult to do before airplanes. Now, we can travel quickly and safely. When people choose how to travel, they should choose to fly!

Andersen Ross/Blend Images/Getty Images

Paragraph 4

How does Darren support his claim that airplanes are the safest way to travel?

_____

_____

_____

_____

Paragraph 5

What sentence in the conclusion restates the supporting reasons Darren gives in the introduction?

_____

_____

_____

_____

_____

Apply the Rubric

With a partner, use the rubric on page 102 to discuss why Darren's essay is successful.

Analyze the Prompt

Writing Prompt

Write an opinion essay arguing for or against the use of self-driving cars.

Purpose, Audience, and Task Reread the writing prompt. What is your purpose for writing? My purpose is to _____

_____

Who will your audience be? My audience will be _____

_____

What type of writing is the prompt asking for? _____

_____

Set a Purpose for Reading Sources Asking questions about the pros and cons of self-driving cars will help you figure out your purpose for reading. It also helps you understand what you already know about the topic. Before you read the passage set about self-driving cars, write a question here.

_____

_____

_____

jirasaki/Shutterstock

Read the following passage set.

GPS

Lidar (light detection and ranging)

Rear camera

Video cameras

Central computer

Distance sensors

DRIVING
TOWARD A FUTURE

Self-driving cars have distance sensors that tell how close objects are to the car.

1   **Self-driving cars will improve transportation as we know it by replacing human drivers.** They are controlled by a computer inside the vehicle. There is no need for a human driver. Companies are working hard to develop these computers on wheels.

2   How do these cars work? Cameras, lidar, and lasers build 3-D maps of a car's surroundings. GPS tells the car where it is and where to go. A computer uses that information to steer the car. These features allow self-driving cars to react faster than human drivers can.

3   The self-driving car business may be booming in a few short years. Sixty-five percent of Americans think most cars will be driverless by the year 2067.

4   We may see many great changes as self-driving cars become the norm. These cars may be able to communicate. This will improve traffic flow. Travel times will shorten. Fewer human drivers would mean fewer accidents. This will be great for America's roadways.

monicaodo/Shutterstock

OPINION ESSAY

FIND TEXT EVIDENCE

Paragraphs 1–3
Read the highlighted claim, or main opinion, of the article.

Underline the evidence in paragraph 2 that supports the opinion that self-driving cars are better than human drivers.

Paragraph 4
How will self-driving cars reduce traffic?

_____

_____

Diagram
What new information about self-driving cars do you learn from the diagram?

_____

_____

📝 **Take Notes** Paraphrase the claim of the source. Give examples of supporting reasons and relevant evidence.

Paragraph 5

How does the highlighted sentence help you understand the author's opinion?

_____

_____

_____

Paragraphs 6–7

What concerns do some people have about driverless cars?

_____

_____

_____

Paragraphs 8–9

Underline the evidence that supports the opinion that computer systems in cars help driving safety.

Take Notes Paraphrase the claim of the source. Give examples of supporting reasons and relevant evidence.

A SAFER WAY TO DRIVE?

5   Most car accidents are caused by human error. Driverless cars could be a solution. If 90 percent of America's cars were driverless, accidents would drop from 6 million per year to 1.3 million. Traffic safety would improve. **But are driverless cars really the best answer to America's traffic safety problems?**

6   There have been serious crashes involving driverless cars. Many feel they are not safe enough for the road. Over half of adults in the U.S. say they would not ride in a driverless vehicle.

7   There are also questions about traffic laws. Right now, laws hold people responsible for accidents. But if a driverless car causes an accident, who is responsible? Laws will need to be changed. Some worry that this process will be too long and complicated.

8   People have doubts about computer-driven vehicles, but computers already play a role in today's cars. When the steering wheel is turned, a computer moves the wheels. Safety systems can help cars stay in the correct lane. They can brake if the car gets too close to something. These aids have made roadways safer.

9   Cars are becoming smarter. They may even get smart enough to drive themselves. But more must be done to earn the public's trust.

DRIVERLESS CARS: NOT SO FAST!

FIND TEXT EVIDENCE

10   Once the stuff of science fiction, self-driving cars are becoming a reality in today's world. But the negative effects of these vehicles outweigh the positive.

11   Driverless cars are not as safe as you think. A computer controls these vehicles. Computers can be hacked. They sometimes get viruses. It's annoying when this happens to your home computer. But it would be very dangerous if this happened to a car with passengers.

12   Repairing a computer-driven car is a complex job. Car mechanics will need special training. A special engineer may be needed to fix computer problems. Repair costs would skyrocket. The cars themselves would also be quite expensive. This is bad news for car owners and shoppers.

13   Self-driving cars would also affect jobs. Up to 5 million jobs would be lost once driverless cars hit the road. This would affect taxi drivers, truckers, bus drivers—anyone who makes a living as a driver.

14   The idea of a driverless future may seem bright. However, the safety risks and economic impact cast a shadow on that future. Humans are not perfect drivers, but computers aren't either. Computers can help humans be better drivers. They should not take the wheel themselves.

Paragraph 10
Underline the claim in paragraph 10.

Paragraph 11
What risk exists for driverless cars that does not exist for human-driven cars?

_____

_____

_____

Paragraphs 12–13
How would self-driving cars be bad for America's economy?

_____

_____

Paragraph 14
Underline the sentence in paragraph 14 that best summarizes the article.

Take Notes Paraphrase the claim of the source. Give examples of supporting reasons and relevant evidence.

My Goal I can synthesize information from three sources.

TAKE NOTES

Read the writing prompt below. Use the three sources, your notes, and the graphic organizer to plan your essay.

Writing Prompt *Write an opinion essay arguing for or against the use of self-driving cars.*

Synthesize Information

Review the relevant evidence you recorded from each source. How does the information support your opinion about self-driving cars? Discuss your ideas with a partner.

CHECK IN 1 2 3 4

Plan: Organize Ideas

Introduction State the opinion	I believe self-driving cars are/are not a good idea.
Body Supporting Claims	One reason for this is . . .
Conclusion Restate the opinion	

Valentain Jevee/Shutterstock

Relevant Evidence		
Source 1	Source 2	Source 3

Draft: Strong Conclusion

Quick Tip

Remember to use facts, details, and definitions related to your topic to fully explain your ideas. Present facts and details in a logical order.

Summarizing Ideas Writers end an opinion essay with a strong conclusion. They restate their opinion and summarize the supporting claims of the text. They often use an interesting ending to help the reader remember what he or she has learned.

Reread the conclusion paragraph of Darren's essay about air travel. With a partner, discuss how the conclusion summarizes Darren's opinion and supporting claims. Write an answer below.

> Air travel connects people and places. This is the greatest benefit of flying. World leaders can meet face-to-face. Emergency workers can rush to places in need. People can travel to new places and learn about different cultures. These things were difficult to do before airplanes. Now, we can travel quickly and safely. When people choose how to travel, they should choose to fly!

_____

_____

_____

Draft Use your graphic organizer and the example above to write your draft in your writer's notebook. Before you start writing, review the rubric on page 102.

CHECK IN 1 2 3 4

Revise: Peer Conferences

Review a Draft Listen carefully as your partner reads his or her draft aloud. Say what you like about the draft. Use these sentence starters to discuss your partner's draft.

I like the reasons you gave to support your claim because . . .
I have a question about . . .
You can make your conclusion stronger by . . .

After you take turns giving each other feedback, write one of your partner's suggestions that you will use in your revision.

_____

_____

Revising Checklist

- [ ] Is the claim of my essay clearly stated in the introduction?
- [ ] Did I provide strong reasons to support my claim?
- [ ] Did I reference sources throughout my essay?
- [ ] Do I have a strong conclusion?
- [ ] Did I check my spelling and punctuation?

Revision After you finish your peer conference, use the Revising Checklist to help you figure out what you can change to make your essay better. After you finish writing your final draft, use the full rubric on pages 244–247 to score your essay.

Turn to page 89. Fill in the bars to show what you learned.

My Score			
Purpose, Focus, & Organization (4 pts)	Evidence & Elaboration (4 pts)	Conventions (2 pts)	Total (10 pts)

My Goal I can read and understand social studies texts.

TAKE NOTES

Take notes and annotate as you read the passage "On the Moon."

Look for the answer to the question. *How was the Moon landing a unique moment in history?*

PASSAGE **1** EXPOSITORY TEXT

ON THE MOON

July 16, 1969, the Apollo 11 mission to the Moon blasts off from Florida's Kennedy Space Center. The crew aboard are Neil Armstrong, Michael Collins, and Edwin "Buzz" Aldrin.

At 9:32 a.m., the Saturn V rocket engines fire. For the first time in history, astronauts are on their way to the Moon!

July 20, Aldrin and Armstrong crawl from the command module, *Columbia*, into the lunar module, *Eagle*. The lunar module is the smaller spacecraft that will land on the Moon. At 1:46 that afternoon, *Eagle* separates from *Columbia*.

By 4:05, Armstrong is looking for a smooth place to land on the Moon. His heartbeat rises from a normal 77 beats to 156!

While Armstrong flies, Aldrin lets him know how close they are: "750 feet . . . 400 feet . . . 75 feet, things looking good . . . . Picking up some dust . . . 30 feet. Okay, engine stop."

At 4:18, Armstrong radios mission control, "The *Eagle* has landed."

The Saturn V rocket was longer than a football field.

Walk on the Moon

At 10:39 that evening, Armstrong is ready to leave the *Eagle*. He opens the hatch and slowly makes his way down the ladder.

Buzz Aldrin climbing down the steps to walk on the Moon.

At 10:56, Armstrong puts his left foot on the Moon. "That's one small step for a man, one giant leap for mankind," Armstrong radios to mission control and the people of Earth. He walks on the Moon and collects rock samples. Armstrong describes the Moon's surface as "fine and powdery. I can kick it up loosely with my toe. It does adhere in fine layers, like powdered charcoal, to the sole and sides of my boots."

He places a plaque on the Moon that reads, "Here men from the planet Earth first set foot on the Moon. July 1969 A.D. We came in peace for all mankind." The astronauts also plant an American flag on the Moon.

The astronauts spend 2 hours and 47 minutes walking on the Moon.

Meanwhile, Collins is all alone on *Columbia,* orbiting the Moon, waiting for his crewmates' return. He is now the most isolated man in the world.

NASA

TAKE NOTES

TAKE NOTES

_____

_____

_____

_____

_____

_____

_____

_____

_____

_____

_____

_____

_____

_____

_____

_____

H○ME

On July 21 at 1:54 p.m., the *Eagle* blasts off from the Moon's surface. It will now reconnect with *Columbia* and Collins, who is still orbiting the Moon. At 5:35, the *Eagle* rejoins *Columbia*.

On July 24 at 12:35, the crew reenters Earth's atmosphere. They are almost home! Minutes later, the spacecraft splashes down close to Hawaii.

The astronauts are placed in quarantine for three days to be sure they haven't returned with any deadly germs from the Moon. No one on Earth knows what they could have brought back.

While waiting, the astronauts watch a tape recording of their Moon landing. Buzz looks at Neil and says, "Hey, we missed the whole thing!"

The lunar module *Eagle* launches from the Moon to rejoin *Columbia*.

NASA-Johnson Space Center Media Archive

CENTRAL IDEA AND RELEVANT DETAILS

Create a central idea chart like the one below. Use it to record the relevant details in the section titled "Walk on the Moon." Use these details to find the central idea, or main idea, of the section.

Detail
Detail
Detail
Central Idea

Synthesize Information

Reread the first paragraph of "On the Moon" and the second paragraph of "Home." How long were the astronauts in space? What can you infer about how far the Moon is from Earth?

CHECK IN   1   2   3   4

WHAT DO YOU REMEMBER?

Plan an Interview You've read about important moments in history and how people remember them. Now it's time to interview someone who has witnessed an important event. For example, you might interview someone who remembers the Apollo 11 Moon landing of 1969.

Work in a group and write four questions to ask a trusted adult about an important event in the past that he or she experienced.

1. _____

2. _____

3. _____

4. _____

Now think about your interview plan. Who will you interview? When will you interview him or her? How will you record the interview? Write your interview plan here.

_____

_____

_____

_____

SUMMARIZE THE INTERVIEW

Look at your notes from the interview. Think about what you learned about an event in history. Write a short summary of the interview. Be sure to include the name of the person you interviewed and facts about the event.

The person I interviewed was _____

_____

The historical event they told me about was _____

_____

This is when the event happened: _____

_____

_____

Summary of the interview: _____

_____

_____

_____

_____

After you finish your summary, discuss with a partner what you learned about a historical event and what the interview inspires you to research or do.

My Goal I can read and understand science texts.

TAKE NOTES

Take notes and annotate as you read the passages "Fascinating Facts About Our Amazing Sun" and "Sun Storms."

Look for the answer to the question. *What do we know about how the Sun affects life on Earth?*

PASSAGE 1

EXPOSITORY TEXT

Fascinating Facts About Our Amazing Sun

If you are like a lot of people, you take the Sun for granted. You might even complain that it is too hot or too bright. But without the Sun, there would be no life on Earth. It gives us light. It keeps us warm. It grows our food. If there were no Sun, Earth would be nothing more than a big ball of ice.

Here are some other fascinating facts about the Sun.

The Sun is the center of our solar system. All eight planets, their moons, and other objects in the solar system orbit, or circle around, the Sun.

The Sun is a star, or a body of hot gases that makes and gives off heat and light energy. This energy provides the light and heat that all life needs to survive on Earth.

The Sun has gravity, or an invisible force that pulls objects toward it. The Sun's gravity holds the solar system together. It keeps everything, from the largest planets to the tiniest pieces of dust, in the Sun's orbit.

The Sun is the largest object in our solar system. It is about one million times bigger than Earth. However, it is not the largest star in the galaxy. It seems extremely big to us because, at 93 million miles away, it is closer to us than any other star.

The Sun also influences the daily rise and fall of ocean waters, weather, climate, and many other natural wonders.

Sunlight can be harmful to your eyes and skin. It is never a good idea to look directly at the Sun, or to be outside too long without protection, such as sunglasses. Applying sunscreen to your skin is also important. Too much sunlight on unprotected skin can lead to serious diseases, including skin cancer.

The Sun contributes to good health, too. It helps the body make vitamin D, which is vital to the body's functions.

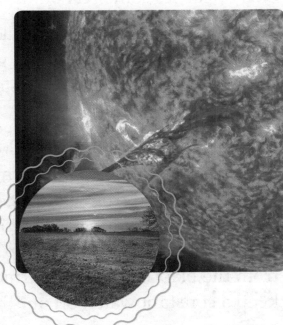

The next time you think the Sun is a bother, remember how important it is to all life on Earth!

TAKE NOTES

SUN STORMS

You know what happens when there is a storm on Earth. It may rain a lot. It may be so windy that trees blow over. But what happens when there is a storm on the Sun?

The Sun doesn't have weather like we do on Earth. A storm on the Sun is caused by exploding magnetic energy. A large explosion shoots energy into space. When the Sun is facing Earth, that energy causes some real damage.

This is a photo of a blast from the Halloween storms of 2003. The photo is colored green so you can clearly see the blast.

The biggest solar storm is called a coronal mass ejection. The massive blast of electrified gas rushes toward Earth at 5 million miles per hour. These storms can cause power outages and damage satellites.

The Halloween storms of 2003 were something special. They were the largest sun storms scientists have observed. The blasts lasted from October to November. The astronauts on the International Space Station were in danger. They took cover deep inside the ship's safety zone. The radiation from the blast could have harmed the astronauts. Scientists keep a constant watch on our Sun so we can stay safe here on Earth. And astronauts can stay safe in space.

NASA/ESA

COMPARE THE PASSAGES

Review your notes from "Fascinating Facts About Our Amazing Sun" and "Sun Storms." Use your notes and a Venn diagram to record how information in the passages is alike and different.

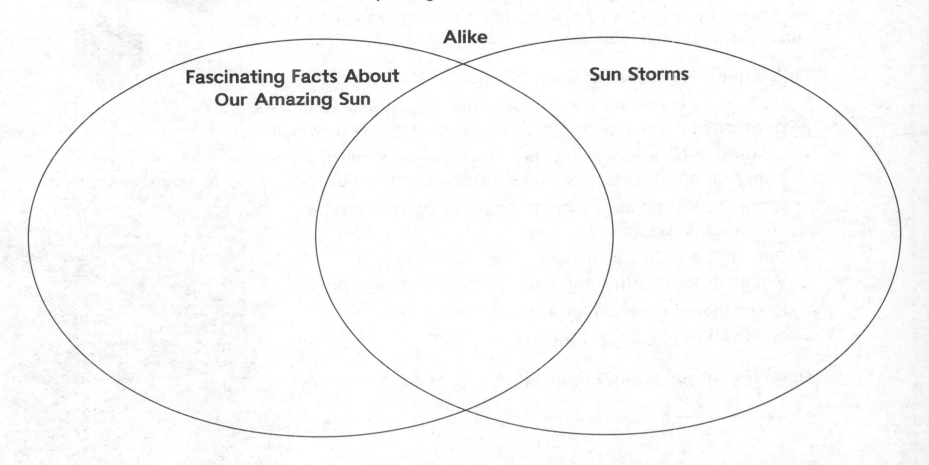

Alike

Fascinating Facts About Our Amazing Sun

Sun Storms

Synthesize Information

Review what you learned about how the Sun affects life on Earth. Why is it important for us to continue studying the Sun?

CHECK IN 1 2 3 4

SCIENCE

EXPLORE SUN PRINTS

The Sun's energy travels 93 million miles to reach the Earth. Without the Sun, there would be no life here on Earth. The Sun's rays may travel a vast distance, but they are still very powerful when they reach Earth. That's why you need to wear sunscreen to protect your skin.

Let's explore the power of the Sun's rays.

- Gather the materials: dark construction paper; leaves, flowers, or other flat items; clear plastic wrap; rocks to use as weights.

- Go outside on a very sunny day. Place the dark construction paper on a flat surface, such as a sidewalk or table.

- Place the flat objects, such as leaves or flowers, on the construction paper.

- Stretch the clear plastic wrap to cover the objects. Weigh it down with small rocks so it doesn't blow away.

- Leave them in the sun for at least three hours.

- Remove the plastic and the items.

Observe your sun prints. Record what happened to the paper.

_____

_____

 Discuss your observations with your partner. Use what you know about the Sun to explain what happened to change the paper.

Reflect on Your Learning

Talk About It Reflect on what you learned in this unit. Then talk with a partner about how you did.

I am really proud of how I can _____

_____

_____

_____

Something I need to work more on is _____

_____

_____

_____

Share a goal you have with a partner.

My Goal Set a goal for Unit 4. In your reader's notebook, write about what you can do to get there.

Build Knowledge

Build Vocabulary

Write new words you learned about how people use their skills and talents to help others. Draw lines and circles for the words you write.

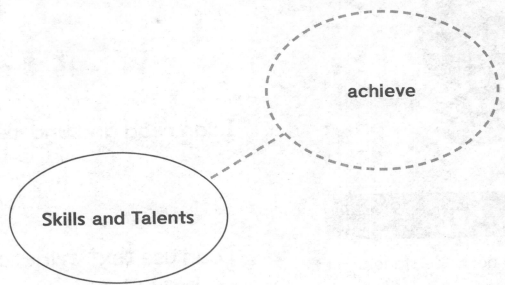

achieve

Skills and Talents

Go online to **my.mheducation.com** and read the "Clara Barton" Blast. Think about why learning about people who help others is important. Then blast back your response.

kali9/iStock/Getty Images

Think about what you already know. Fill in the bars. This will be a good start.

What I Know Now

I can read and understand realistic fiction.

I can use text evidence to respond to realistic fiction.

| 1 | 2 | 3 | 4 |

I know how we can use what we know to help others.

Key			
1 =	I do not understand.		
2 =	I understand but need more practice.		
3 =	I understand.		
4 =	I understand and can teach someone.		

STOP You will come back to the next page later.

Think about what you learned. Fill in the bars. What are you getting better at?

What I Learned

I can read and understand realistic fiction.

1 > 2 > 3 > 4

I can use text evidence to respond to realistic fiction.

1 > 2 > 3 > 4

I know how we can use what we know to help others.

1 > 2 > 3 > 4

My Goal I can read and understand realistic fiction.

TAKE NOTES

As you read, make note of interesting words and important events.

_____

_____

_____

_____

_____

_____

_____

_____

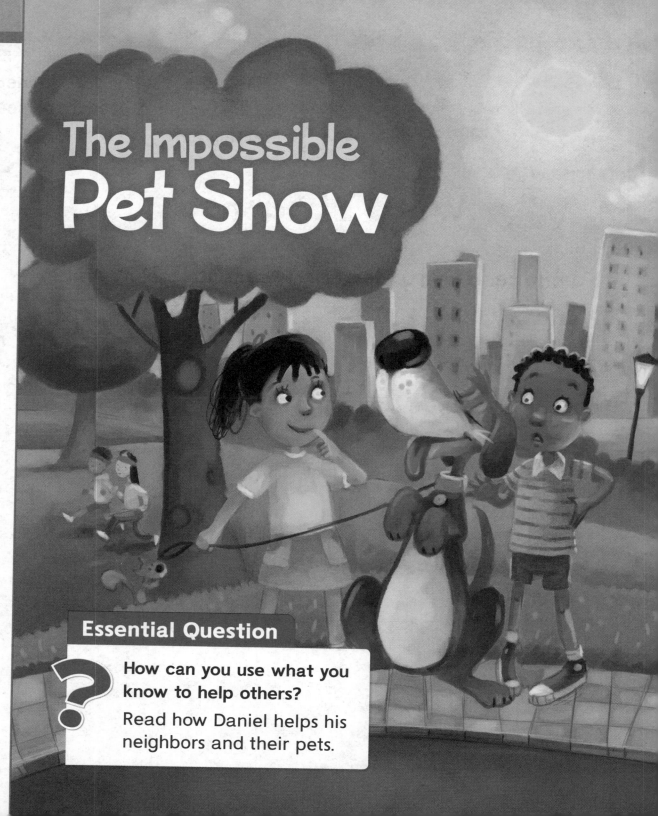

The Impossible Pet Show

Essential Question

? How can you use what you know to help others?

Read how Daniel helps his neighbors and their pets.

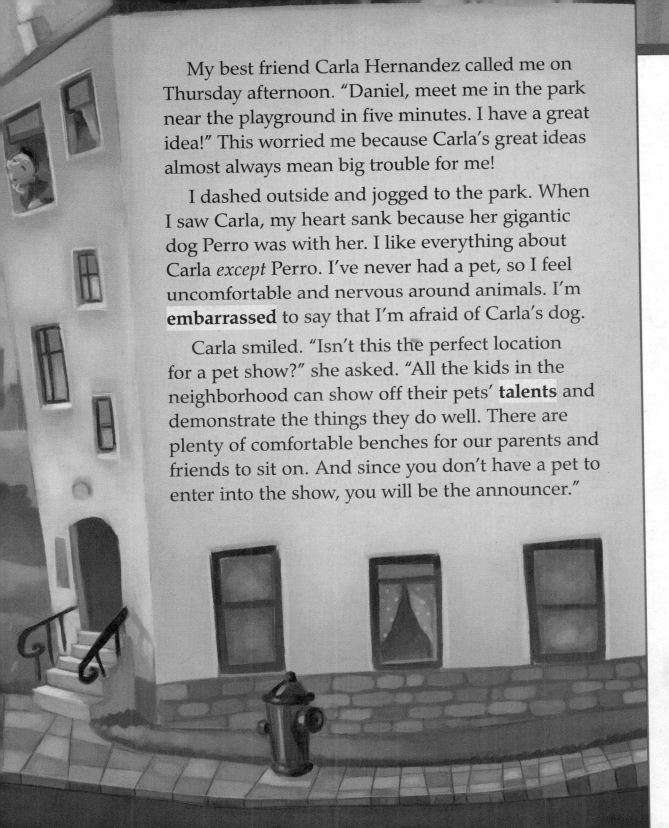

My best friend Carla Hernandez called me on Thursday afternoon. "Daniel, meet me in the park near the playground in five minutes. I have a great idea!" This worried me because Carla's great ideas almost always mean big trouble for me!

I dashed outside and jogged to the park. When I saw Carla, my heart sank because her gigantic dog Perro was with her. I like everything about Carla *except* Perro. I've never had a pet, so I feel uncomfortable and nervous around animals. I'm **embarrassed** to say that I'm afraid of Carla's dog.

Carla smiled. "Isn't this the perfect location for a pet show?" she asked. "All the kids in the neighborhood can show off their pets' **talents** and demonstrate the things they do well. There are plenty of comfortable benches for our parents and friends to sit on. And since you don't have a pet to enter into the show, you will be the announcer."

FIND TEXT EVIDENCE

Read

Paragraph 1

Ask and Answer Questions

Why is Daniel worried after getting a call from his best friend Carla? **Underline** text evidence.

Paragraph 2

Plot: Character Development

Circle text evidence that shows how Daniel reacts when he sees Carla. Why does he act this way?

_____

_____

_____

Paragraph 3

Character Perspective

Draw a box around Carla's dialogue that tells why she thinks Daniel should be the announcer.

Reread

Author's Craft

How does the author help you understand what the phrase "my heart sank" means?

FIND TEXT EVIDENCE

Read

Paragraphs 1–2
Prefixes
Find the word *nonsense*. **Circle** the prefix. Use the prefix to figure out the meaning of the word. Write the meaning here.

_____

_____

Paragraphs 3–5
Plot: Character Development
Why is Daniel nervous the morning of the pet show? How does he change after the show begins? **Underline** text evidence.

_____

_____

Reread

Author's Craft

How does the author help you understand how Daniel feels on Saturday morning?

"I'm sorry," I **apologized**, "but that's impossible! Crowds make me nervous and unsure. Besides, I don't like animals, remember?"

"That's nonsense," said Carla. "There's nothing to be concerned about because you'll be great!"

Just then, Perro leaped up, slobbered all over me, and almost knocked me down. "Yuck. Down, Perro! Stay!" I shouted. Perro sat as still as a statue. "Wow, you're good at that," said Carla. "Now let's get started, because we have a lot to do."

By Saturday morning I had practiced announcing each pet's act a hundred times. My stomach was doing flip flops by the time the **audience** arrived. The size of the crowd made me feel even more anxious.

When the show began, I gulped and announced the first pet. It was a parakeet named Butter whose talent was walking back and forth on a wire. When Butter finished, everyone clapped and cheered. So far, everything was perfect, and I was beginning to feel calmer and more relaxed. I **realized** that being an announcer wasn't so bad after all.

Then it was Carla and Perro's turn.

"Sit, Perro," she said, but Perro didn't sit.

Perro was not paying **attention** to Carla. He was too interested in watching Jack's bunnies jump in and out of their boxes. Suddenly, Perro leaped at the bunnies who hopped toward Mandy and knocked over her hamster's cage. Pudgy, the hamster, escaped and began running around in circles while Kyle's dog, Jake, howled. This was a disaster, and I had to do something.

"Sit!" I shouted at Perro. "Quiet!" I ordered Jake. "Stay!" I yelled. Everyone—kids and pets—stopped and stared at me. Even the audience froze.

"Daniel, that was incredible," said Carla. "You got the pets to settle down. That's quite an **achievement**."

Sadly, that was the end of our pet show. But now I have more **confidence** when I have to speak in front of people. And even though I am still nervous around animals, Perro and I have become great friends. And I've discovered my talent, too.

Summarize

Use your notes and think about what happened in "The Impossible Pet Show." Use the plot and theme to summarize the text.

FIND TEXT EVIDENCE

Read

Paragraphs 1–5
Character Perspective

How does Carla feel about how Daniel got everyone's pets under control? **Underline** text evidence.

_____

_____

Paragraph 6
Plot: Character Development

How does Daniel feel about crowds after the pet show? How does he feel about Perro? **Circle** text evidence.

_____

_____

_____

Reread

Author's Craft

How does the author help you understand Daniel's talent?

Vocabulary

Use the sentences to talk with a partner about each word. Then answer the questions.

achievement

It is a big **achievement** to fly a kite on a very windy day.

What is your biggest achievement?

_____

_____

apologized

Kate **apologized** for breaking the dish.

When have you apologized for doing something?

_____

_____

> **Build Your Word List** Reread page 132. Draw a box around a word you think is interesting. Use a dictionary to look up the word's meaning. Write the word and its definition in your reader's notebook.

attention

It is important to pay **attention** to directions.

How do you show your teacher you are paying attention in class?

_____

_____

audience

The **audience** clapped and cheered at the end of the play.

When have you been part of an audience?

_____

_____

confidence

Jody read her report calmly and with **confidence**.

What does it mean to have confidence?

_____

_____

embarrassed

Tia was **embarrassed** when she forgot her lines in the play.

When have you felt embarrassed?

_____

_____

realized

My soccer team celebrated when we **realized** we had won the game.

Describe a time when you realized something.

_____

_____

talents

One of Lila's **talents** is playing the violin.

What is one of your talents?

_____

_____

Prefixes

A prefix is a word part added to the beginning of a word. A prefix changes the word's meaning. The prefixes _un-, non-,_ and _im-_ mean "not" or "opposite of."

🔍 FIND TEXT EVIDENCE

On page 132, I see the word unsure. _It has the base word_ sure _and the prefix_ un-. _I know that_ sure _means "certain" and the prefix_ un- _means "not." The word_ unsure _must mean "not certain."_

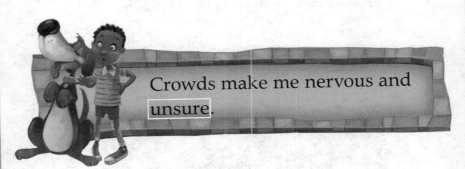

Crowds make me nervous and unsure.

Your Turn Use your knowledge of prefixes and base words to figure out each word's meaning.

uncomfortable, page 131 _____

impossible, page 132 _____

CHECK IN ⟩ 1 ⟩ 2 ⟩ 3 ⟩ 4 ⟩

Ask and Answer Questions

Ask yourself questions about "The Impossible Pet Show" as you read. Then look for details to answer your questions. This helps you deepen your understanding of a text.

FIND TEXT EVIDENCE

Look at page 132. Ask a question about what is happening. Then read again to find the answer.

Page 132

When the show began, I gulped and announced the first pet. It was a parakeet named Butter whose talent was walking back and forth on a wire. When Butter finished, everyone clapped and cheered. So far, everything was perfect, and I was beginning to feel calmer and more relaxed. I **realized** that being an announcer wasn't so bad after all.

I'm not sure why Daniel thinks being an announcer isn't so bad. <u>After the first act, the audience claps and cheers. Daniel says everything was perfect.</u> Now I understand that Daniel doesn't think being an announcer is so bad because the show is going well and he's becoming more comfortable.

Your Turn With a partner, think of another question to ask about "The Impossible Pet Show." You might ask why Daniel thinks the pet show turns into a disaster. Reread page 133 to find the answer.

_____

_____

CHECK IN 〉 1 〉 2 〉 3 〉 4

Character Perspective

"The Impossible Pet Show" is **realistic fiction**. Realistic fiction

- has a made-up plot, or story events, that could really happen
- has characters who may share their perspectives through dialogue
- may be part of a longer book with chapters or part of a series about the same characters

🔍 FIND TEXT EVIDENCE

"The Impossible Pet Show" is realistic fiction. The characters talk and act like real people. They share their perspectives. The events are made up, but they could really happen.

Readers to Writers

Reread the dialogue on page 132. How does it help you understand the characters?

When you write realistic fiction, think about how you can use dialogue to show how each character feels.

Page 132

"I'm sorry," I **apologized**, "but that's impossible! Crowds make me nervous and unsure. Besides, I don't like animals, remember?"

"That's nonsense," said Carla. "There's nothing to be concerned about because you'll be great!"

Just then, Perro leaped up, slobbered all over me, and almost knocked me down. "Yuck. Down, Perro! Stay!" I shouted. Perro sat as still as a statue. "Wow, you're good at that," said Carla. "Now let's get started, because we have a lot to do."

By Saturday morning I had practiced announcing each pet's act a hundred times. My stomach was doing flip flops by the time the **audience** arrived. The size of the crowd made me feel even more anxious.

When the show began, I gulped and announced the first pet. It was a parakeet named Butter whose talent was walking back and forth on a wire. When Butter finished, everyone clapped and cheered. So far, everything was perfect, and I was beginning to feel calmer and more relaxed. I **realized** that being an announcer wasn't so bad after all.

Character Perspective

Perspective refers to a character's thoughts or feelings about something. Characters can show their perspectives through what they say and do.

COLLABORATE

Your Turn Reread the first two paragraphs on page 132 with a partner. How are Daniel's and Carla's perspectives different?

_____

_____

_____

CHECK IN 1 2 3 4

Plot: Character Development

Characters in fiction change throughout a story. The experiences they have may teach them lessons or change their perspectives. This is called character development. To see how characters develop, compare and contrast their traits, feelings, and responses to situations in the beginning, middle, and end of the story.

Quick Tip

A trait is a quality of a character's personality. For example, characters may be honest, shy, kind, or brave. A trait is not the same thing as a feeling. Excitement and hunger, for example, are not character traits.

FIND TEXT EVIDENCE

In the beginning of "The Impossible Pet Show," Daniel is nervous around crowds and animals. I read on to see how Daniel develops.

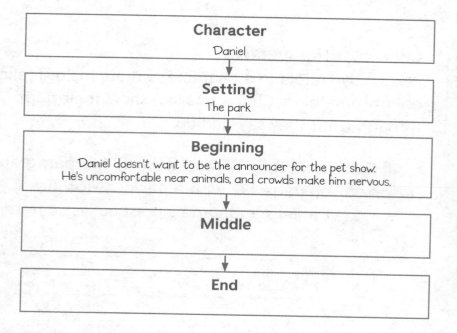

Character
Daniel

↓

Setting
The park

↓

Beginning
Daniel doesn't want to be the announcer for the pet show. He's uncomfortable near animals, and crowds make him nervous.

↓

Middle

↓

End

 Your Turn Reread "The Impossible Pet Show." Complete the graphic organizer with details about Daniel's traits, feelings, and actions in the middle and end of the story. How does Daniel change?

CHECK IN 〉 1 〉 2 〉 3 〉 4 〉

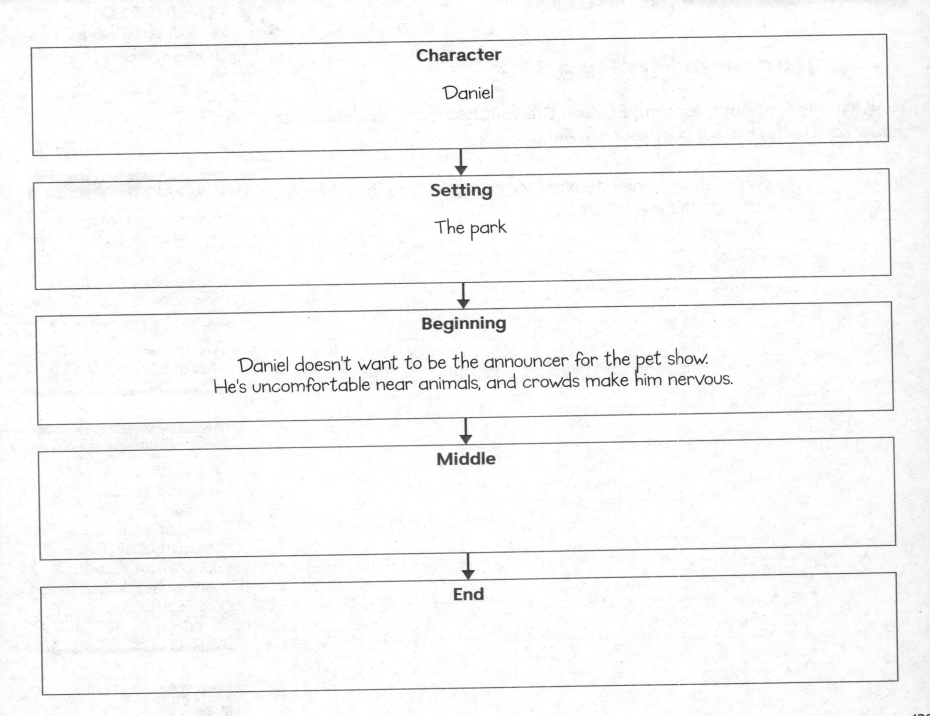

Character

Daniel

Setting

The park

Beginning

Daniel doesn't want to be the announcer for the pet show.
He's uncomfortable near animals, and crowds make him nervous.

Middle

End

My Goal I can use text evidence to respond to realistic fiction.

Respond to Reading

Talk about the prompt below. Use your notes and evidence from the text to support your answer.

Why do you think Daniel develops, or changes, from the beginning of the story to the end?

_____

_____

_____

_____

_____

_____

_____

_____

_____

Quick Tip

Use these sentence starters to talk about how Daniel changes.

In the beginning of the story, Daniel is . . .

At the end, Daniel is . . .

Daniel develops because . . .

Grammar Connections

As you write your response, be sure to use both simple and compound sentences. Use coordinating conjunctions to form compound subjects, predicates, and sentences.

CHECK IN 1 > 2 > 3 > 4

Skills and Talents

Everyone has skills and talents that can be used to help others. What are some of yours? Talk with a partner about some of your skills and talents. Then choose one and follow the research process to write a blog article about it.

Step 1 **Set a Goal** After talking with your partner, choose one of your talents or skills to research.

Step 2 **Identify Sources** Find books and reliable websites with information about your skill or talent. Try to find at least three sources.

Step 3 **Find and Record Information** Think of questions to ask about your skill or talent. For example, you might ask about its history, or about how people learn to do it. Find information in your sources that answers your questions. Record your sources on a Works Cited page. You can use the sample on this page as a model.

Step 4 **Organize and Combine Information** Organize your notes by choosing what facts you want to include in your blog.

Step 5 **Create and Present** Write your blog article about your skill or talent. Include information you found in your sources. Describe how your skill or talent can be used to help others. Share your article with the class.

> **Quick Tip**
>
> A Works Cited page is a list of sources you used for research. Each entry includes the author, title, and publication information of the source.

> **Works Cited**
>
> "Ancient Board Games." *Encyclopedia of Games Online.* Bonus Point Publications, 2011. Web. Feb. 11, 2015.
>
> Baxter, Barry. *The History of Board Games.* Denver: Checkers Press, 2014. Print

CHECK IN 1 > 2 > 3 > 4

The Talented Clementine

? How does the author help you understand how Margaret's teacher and Mrs. Rice are different?

Literature Anthology: pages 278–295

Talk About It Reread paragraphs 3 and 4 on **Literature Anthology** page 284. Talk about what Margaret's teacher and Mrs. Rice do.

Cite Text Evidence What do Margaret's teacher and Mrs. Rice do and say that show how they are different? Write text evidence here.

Clues	How They Are Different

Make Inferences

Use text evidence and what you know to make an inference about how Margaret's teacher and Mrs. Rice feel about Clementine. What does it mean if someone gives a thumbs-up?

Write I know that Margaret's teacher and Mrs. Rice are different

_____

_____

CHECK IN 1 2 3 4

? **How does the author use humor to describe how important Clementine is to the talent show?**

COLLABORATE

Talk About It Reread **Literature Anthology** page 291. Talk about how Clementine describes what's happening onstage.

Cite Text Evidence What words and phrases show that what happens is funny? Write evidence and tell how that helps you see how important Clementine is to the show.

Quick Tip

You can use these sentence starters to talk about how the author uses humor.

The author's description is funny because . . .

I read that Clementine . . .

```
Clue



        ↓
Clue



        ↓
Clue



        ↓
What Connects the Clues


```

Write The author uses humor to _____

_____

? How does the author help you understand what Mrs. Rice means when she tells Clementine that she is "one of a kind"?

Quick Tip

When you reread, you can use nearby words and phrases to help you understand what the author means.

COLLABORATE

Talk About It Reread the last two paragraphs on **Literature Anthology** page 294. Talk with a partner about what Mrs. Rice says to Clementine and how it makes her feel.

Cite Text Evidence What clues help you understand what "one of a kind" means? Write text evidence in the chart.

Text Evidence	How It Helps

Write I understand what "one of a kind" means because the author

_____

_____

_____

CHECK IN 1 2 3 4

Respond to Reading

COLLABORATE

Talk about the prompt below. Use your notes and evidence from the text to support your answer.

Why do you think Clementine develops, or changes, from the beginning of the story to the end?

_____

_____

_____

_____

_____

_____

_____

_____

_____

_____

Quick Tip

Use these sentence starters to talk about how Clementine develops.

In the beginning of the story, Clementine is . . .

By the end, Clementine is . . .

Clementine changes because . . .

CHECK IN 1 > 2 > 3 > 4 >

Clementine and the Family Meeting

Literature Anthology:
pages 298–303

? **How does the author help you understand how Clementine feels about the family meeting?**

Talk About It Reread **Literature Anthology** page 299. Talk with a partner about why Clementine is nervous about the family meeting.

Cite Text Evidence What words and phrases help you understand how Clementine feels? Write text evidence in the chart.

Quick Tip

When you reread, you can use the author's words and phrases to help you understand how the characters feel.

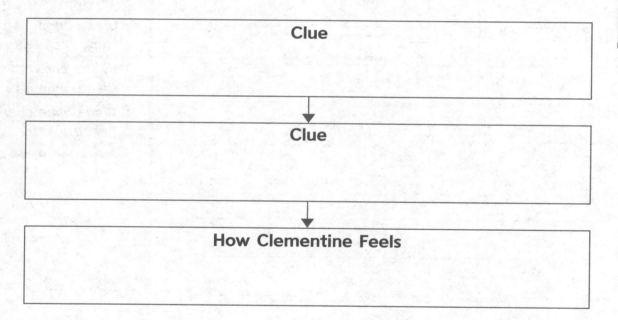

Clue

↓

Clue

↓

How Clementine Feels

Write The author helps me understand how Clementine feels by

_____

_____

CHECK IN 1 2 3 4

? How does the author use illustrations to help you understand
how Clementine feels?

COLLABORATE

Talk About It Look at the illustration on **Literature Anthology**
page 301. Talk about how it adds meaning to the story. What does it
show about Clementine's feelings?

Cite Text Evidence What clues in the illustration help you
understand how Clementine feels? Write them here.

Clues	How Clementine Feels

Write The illustration helps me understand how Clementine feels

_____

_____

_____

_____

Quick Tip

You can use these
sentence starters to talk
about the illustration.

*The illustration shows
Clementine . . .*

*This helps me
understand that she
feels . . .*

How do you know how Clementine feels about having a new baby in the family?

COLLABORATE

Talk About It Reread paragraph 3 on **Literature Anthology** page 302. Talk about what Clementine says.

Cite Text Evidence What words and phrases help you know how she feels about having a new baby in the family? Write them here.

Quick Tip

Read Clementine's dialogue to understand more about her perspective, or feelings.

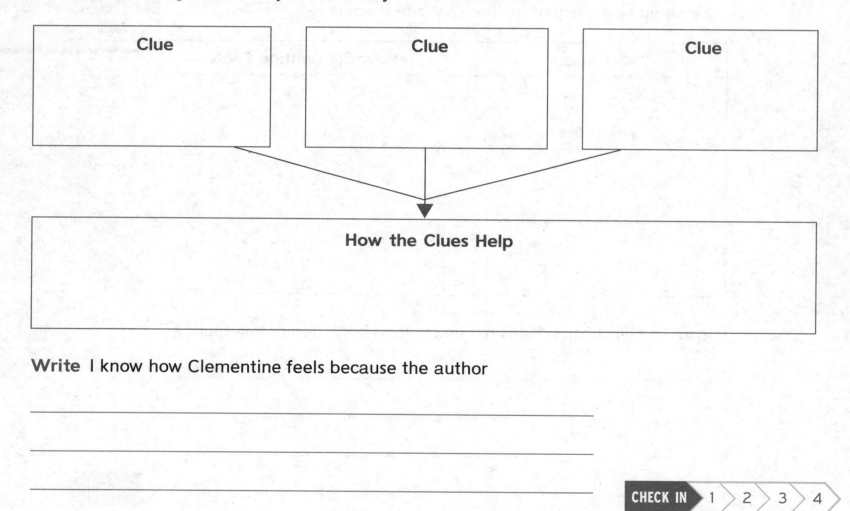

Clue	Clue	Clue

How the Clues Help

Write I know how Clementine feels because the author

_____

_____

_____

CHECK IN 1 2 3 4

Figurative Language

Writers use figurative language to make their descriptions more interesting. Figurative language is words or phrases that mean something other than their literal meaning. Two kinds of figurative language are simile and hyperbole. A simile compares two things with the words *like* or *as*. Hyperbole is an obvious exaggeration.

FIND TEXT EVIDENCE

On page 302 of Clementine and the Family Meeting *in the* **Literature Anthology,** *Clementine says her little brother is "like a personal-size tornado." Clementine's brother isn't really a tornado. This is a simile that compares him to a tornado because he's made a mess. On the next page, the author describes the kitchen as "tornadoed." This is hyperbole. The author is exaggerating and using humor to show how messy the kitchen is.*

Your Turn Reread the first paragraph on page 300.

- Find an example of figurative language and write it below.

_____

- Is the example you found a simile or hyperbole? What does it

help you picture in your mind? _____

_____

MAKE CONNECTIONS

? **How do the photograph and** *The Talented Clementine* **show how you can help others?**

Talk About It Look at the photograph and read the caption. With a partner, talk about what the girls are doing.

Cite Text Evidence **Circle** details in the photograph that show what each girl's talent is. Then **underline** the text evidence in the caption that tells what they are doing. Above the photograph, tell how the girls feel. **Draw a box around** evidence in the photograph that supports your answer.

Write The photograph and *The Talented Clementine*

help me understand _____

_____

_____

_____

_____

_____

_____

Quick Tip

Use what you see in the photograph to understand the theme. This will help you compare it to a text.

Janey and Lucretia practice one hour a day. They are performing in a talent show and want to win.

CHECK IN 1 > 2 > 3 > 4

Write a Newspaper Op-Ed

Think over what you learned about how people use their skills and talents to help others. What are the benefits of helping others? Why is it important to help people?

1. Look at your Build Knowledge notes in your reader's notebook.

2. Write an op-ed, or opinion article, for a school newspaper. In your op-ed, tell the reader why helping others is important. Describe the good things that can happen when you help others. Use examples from the texts you read to support your ideas. Include new vocabulary words you learned in your writing.

3. Add a headline, or title, to your op-ed.

Think about what you learned in this text set. Fill in the bars on page 129.

Build Knowledge

Build Vocabulary

Write new words you learned about animals and their adaptations. Draw lines and circles for the words you write.

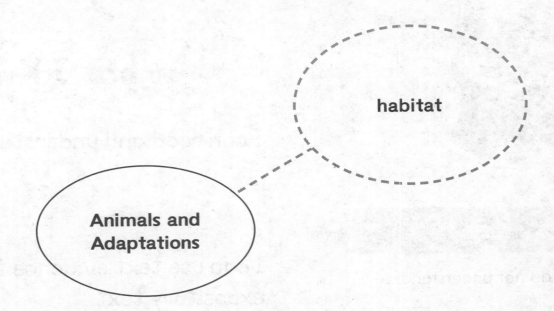

habitat

Animals and Adaptations

BLAST BACK! studysync®

Go online to **my.mheducation.com** and read the "Creatures of the Deep" Blast. Think about why learning about animals is important. Then blast back your response.

Think about what you already know. Fill in the bars. It's okay if you want more practice.

What I Know Now

Key

1 = I do not understand.

2 = I understand but need more practice.

3 = I understand.

4 = I understand and can teach someone.

I can read and understand expository text.

> 1 > 2 > 3 > 4 >

I can use text evidence to respond to expository text.

> 1 > 2 > 3 > 4 >

I know how animals adapt to challenges in their habitat.

> 1 > 2 > 3 > 4 >

STOP You will come back to the next page later.

Think about what you learned. Fill in the bars. What progress did you make?

What I Learned

I can read and understand expository text.

1 > 2 > 3 > 4

I can use text evidence to respond to expository text.

1 > 2 > 3 > 4

I know how animals adapt to challenges in their habitat.

1 > 2 > 3 > 4

My Goal: I can read and understand expository text.

TAKE NOTES

As you read, make note of interesting words and important information.

GRAY WOLF! RED FOX!

Essential Question

How do animals adapt to challenges in their habitat?

Read how gray wolves and red foxes adapt to challenges.

Did you ever see a photograph of a gray wolf or a red fox? Don't they look a lot like dogs? Aren't they fantastic-looking animals? Well, dogs, foxes, and wolves are all **related**. They are all members of the same family. And while gray wolves and red foxes might look alike, they are different in many ways.

LOOKS ARE EVERYTHING

The gray wolf is the largest member, or a part, of the wild dog family. An adult wolf is the size of a large dog. The red fox is smaller and weighs less. Both animals have **excellent** hearing. The red fox can even hear small animals digging holes underground.

And just take a look at those beautiful tails! The gray wolf and red fox both have long, bushy tails. The wolf's tail can be two feet long. The fox's tail is not as long but has a bright, white tip. In the winter, foxes use their thick, furry tails as **protection** from the cold.

The gray wolf and red fox are both mammals.

FIND TEXT EVIDENCE

Read

Paragraph 1
Reread
What animals are foxes related to?

Draw a box around text evidence to support your answer.

Paragraphs 2–3
Compare and Contrast
How is the gray wolf like a dog? **Underline** text evidence.

Captions

What new information did you learn about the gray wolf and red fox in the caption?

Reread

Author's Craft

Why is "Looks Are Everything" a good heading?

SHARED READ

FIND TEXT EVIDENCE

Read

Maps

Circle places on the map where both red foxes and gray wolves live. Use the legend, or key.

Paragraph 1

Compare and Contrast

Underline how a wolf's fur and a fox's fur are the same.

Paragraph 2

Sentence Clues

Draw a box around clues that tell what *habitats* are.

Paragraph 3

Reread

Why don't foxes and wolves compete for food?

Reread

Author's Craft

How does the author use words and phrases to help you visualize what red foxes do to get food?

Foxes and wolves also have thick fur. Their coats can be white, brown, or black. However, red foxes most often have red fur, while a gray wolf's fur is usually more gray and brown.

FINDING FOOD

Gray wolves and red foxes live in many different habitats. They live in forests, deserts, woodlands, and grasslands. But as more people build roads and shopping centers, both animals have lost their homes. The red fox has adapted well, or made changes to fit into its **environment**. Now more foxes make their homes close to towns and parks. Wolves, however, stay far away from towns and people.

Foxes and wolves are not in **competition** for food. They have different diets. Red foxes **prefer** to hunt alone and eat small animals, birds, and fish. They also like to raid garbage cans and campsites for food. Wolves work together in packs, or groups, to hunt large animals, such as moose and deer.

WHERE DO THEY LIVE?

LEGEND
- Red fox only
- Gray wolf only
- Both

Gray wolves prefer to live and hunt in packs.

DAY-TO-DAY

Wolves live in packs of four to seven. They do almost everything together. They hunt, travel, and choose safe places to set up dens for **shelter**. Foxes, on the other hand, like to live alone. They usually sleep in the open or find an empty hole to call home.

The red fox hunts for food alone.

Both wolves and foxes communicate by barking and growling. The gray wolf also howls to **alert**, or warn, other wolves when there is danger nearby. The red fox signals in a different way. It waves its tail in the air to caution other foxes.

The gray wolf and red fox are members of the same family and have many things in common. But they really are two very different animals.

Summarize

Use your notes and think about the comparisons made in "Gray Wolf! Red Fox!" Summarize the text using the central idea and relevant details.

(t)Mapping Specialists, Ltd.; (b)Jeff Vanuga/Corbis/Getty Images; (tr)jimkruger/iStock/Getty Images; (twigs)McGraw-Hill Education

EXPOSITORY TEXT

FIND TEXT EVIDENCE 🔍

Read

Paragraph 1

Compare and Contrast

Underline text evidence that shows what's different about where wolves and foxes live.

Paragraphs 2–3

Sentence Clues

What clues help you figure out what *signals* means?

_____

Reread

What are three things wolves do to communicate?

_____

_____

_____

Reread

Author's Craft

How do you know how the author feels about the gray wolf and the red fox?

Vocabulary

Use the sentences to talk with a partner about each word. Then answer the questions.

alert

Wolves howl to **alert** other wolves when danger is nearby.

How would you alert someone to talk quietly?

_____

_____

competition

Nathan won the **competition** because he was the fastest runner.

What kind of competition have you participated in?

_____

_____

> **Build Your Word List** Reread paragraph 3 on page 157. Draw a box around the word *protection*. In your reader's notebook, use a word web to write more forms of the word. Use a dictionary to help you.

environment

The polar bear lives in a cold and snowy **environment**.

Describe a whale's environment.

_____

_____

excellent

Lily's **excellent** artwork won first place in the art show.

Describe something you did that was excellent.

_____

_____

prefer

Andre and his friends **prefer** walking to riding their bikes.

What kind of transportation do you prefer?

_____

_____

protection

The skunk's scent provides **protection** from its enemies.

What do you use for protection on sunny days?

_____

_____

related

Josh and Jen are **related** because they are both members of the same family.

What are two animals that are related?

_____

_____

shelter

Our tent was a dry and safe **shelter** during the storm.

What is another kind of shelter people use?

_____

_____

Sentence Clues

Sentence clues are words within a sentence or in a nearby sentence that help you figure out the meaning of an unfamiliar word. Sometimes clues define, or tell exactly, what a word means.

🔍 FIND TEXT EVIDENCE

I'm not sure what the word member *means on page 157. I see the words* or a part *in the same sentence. This clue tells me that* member *means "a part of something."*

The gray wolf is the largest member, or a part, of the wild dog family.

Your Turn Use sentence clues to figure out the meanings of these words.

adapted, page 158 _____

packs, page 158 _____

Talk about the sentence clues that helped you figure out the meanings.

CHECK IN ▶ 1 ⟩ 2 ⟩ 3 ⟩ 4 ⟩

James Hager/robertharding/Getty Images

Reread

Stop and think about the text as you read. Are there new facts and ideas? Do they make sense? Reread to make sure you understand.

 FIND TEXT EVIDENCE

Do you understand how fox fur is like wolf fur? Reread the first paragraph on page 158.

Page 158

Foxes and wolves also have thick fur. Their coats can be white, brown, or black. However, red foxes most often have red fur, while a gray wolf's fur is usually more gray and brown.

WHERE

I read that foxes and wolves both have thick fur. I also read that their coats can be white, brown, or black. Now I understand some of the ways fox fur is like wolf fur.

Your Turn Reread "Day-to-Day" on page 159. Do you understand the difference between how wolves and foxes communicate? With a partner, find text evidence about how wolves and foxes communicate in different ways. Then write the answer below.

_____

_____

CHECK IN   1   2   3   4

Maps and Captions

"Gray Wolf! Red Fox!" is an **expository text**. Expository text

- is written by an author to inform readers about a topic
- gives facts and information to explain a topic
- includes text features, such as maps, photographs, and captions

🔍 FIND TEXT EVIDENCE

I can tell that "Gray Wolf! Red Fox!" is an expository text. It explains how gray wolves and red foxes are alike and different. It includes a map, photographs, and captions to better inform the reader.

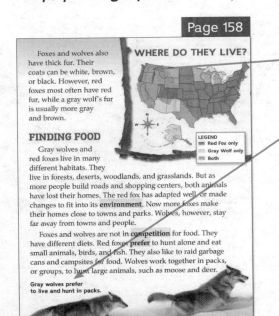

Page 158

Foxes and wolves also have thick fur. Their coats can be white, brown, or black. However, red foxes most often have red fur, while a gray wolf's fur is usually more gray and brown.

FINDING FOOD

Gray wolves and red foxes live in many different habitats. They live in forests, deserts, woodlands, and grasslands. But as more people build roads and shopping centers, both animals have lost their homes. The red fox has adapted well or made changes to fit into its **environment**. Now more foxes make their homes close to towns and parks. Wolves, however, stay far away from towns and people.

Foxes and wolves are not in **competition** for food. They have different diets. Red foxes **prefer** to hunt alone and eat small animals, birds, and fish. They also like to raid garbage cans and campsites for food. Wolves work together in packs, or groups, to hunt large animals, such as moose and deer.

Gray wolves prefer to live and hunt in packs.

WHERE DO THEY LIVE?

LEGEND
■ Red Fox only
■ Gray Wolf only
■ Both

Maps

A map is a flat drawing of a place. It has a legend, or key, that shows what colors and symbols mean.

Captions

A caption explains a photograph or illustration. It sometimes gives more information about a topic.

COLLABORATE

Your Turn Look at the text features in "Gray Wolf! Red Fox!" Talk about how the text features support the author's purpose. What is something you learned from them?

_____

_____

_____

CHECK IN ▷ 1 〉 2 〉 3 〉 4

Compare and Contrast

Authors can use a compare-and-contrast text structure to help readers understand what two things do and do not have in common. When authors compare, they show how two things are alike. When they contrast, they show how two things are different.

 FIND TEXT EVIDENCE

How are red foxes and gray wolves alike and different? I can reread paragraph 2 on page 157 of "Gray Wolf! Red Fox!" to find out.

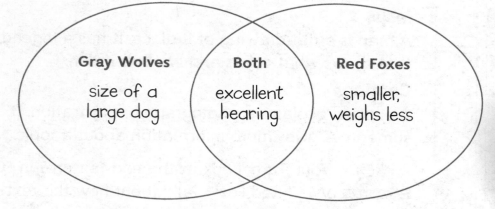

Gray Wolves	Both	Red Foxes
size of a large dog	excellent hearing	smaller, weighs less

 Your Turn Reread the rest of "Gray Wolf! Red Fox!" Find details that tell how red foxes and gray wolves are alike and different. Add these details to your graphic organizer.

CHECK IN 1 2 3 4

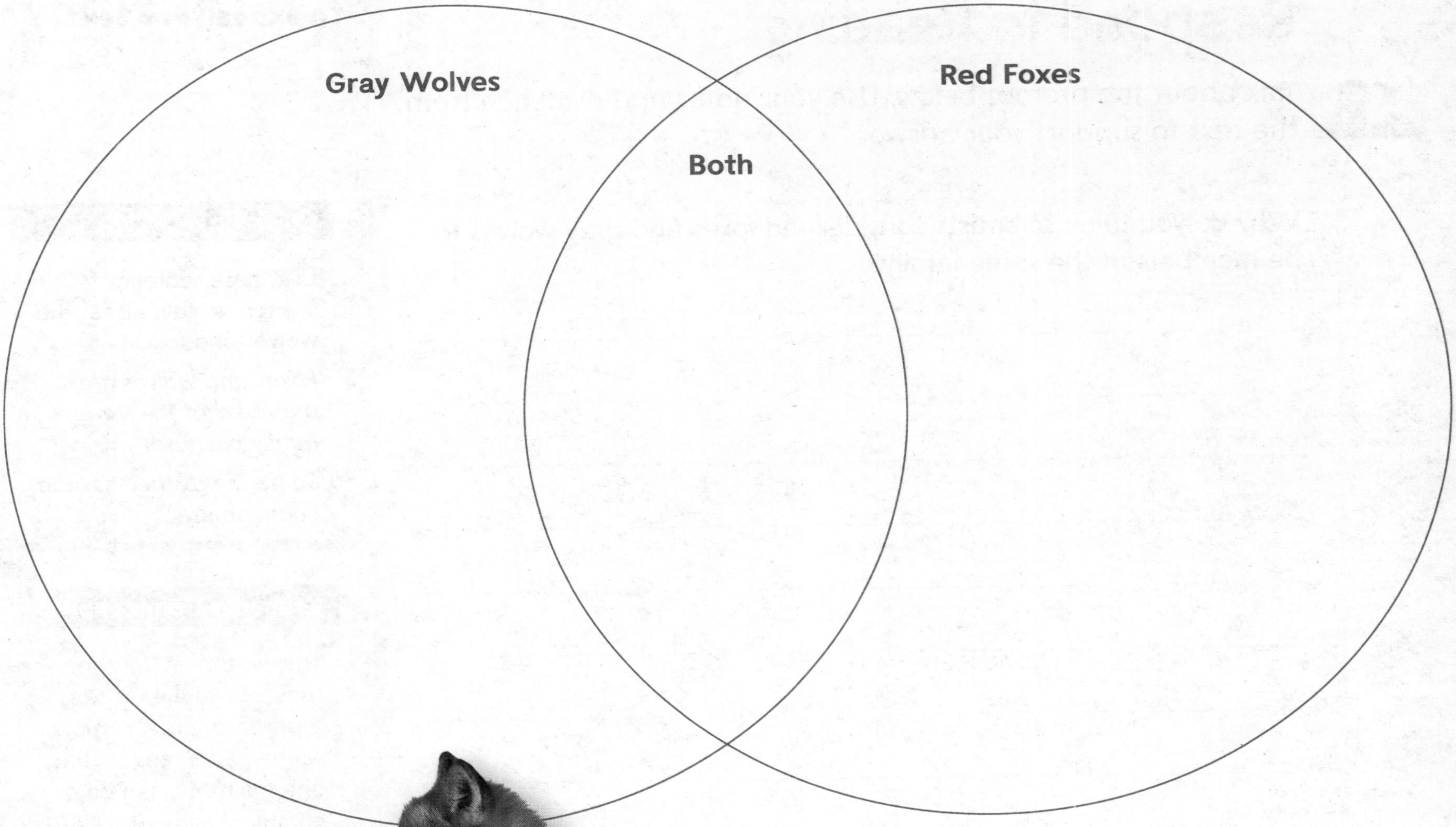

Gray Wolves

Both

Red Foxes

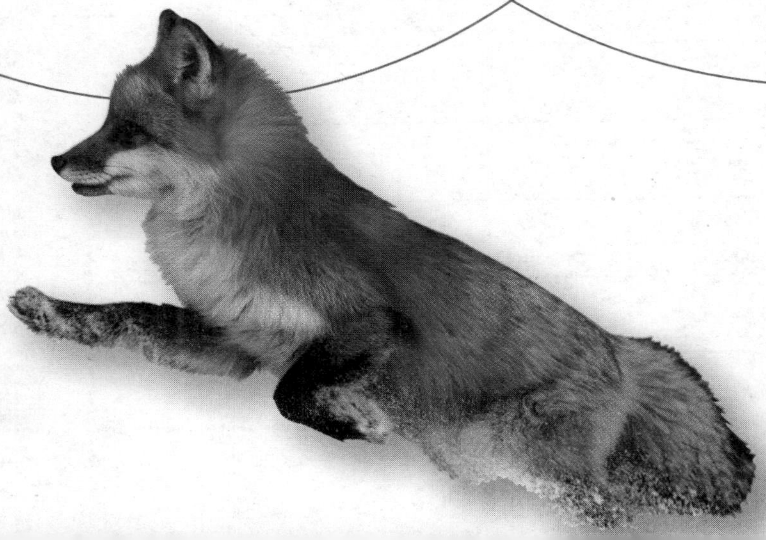

jimkruger/iStock/Getty Images

My Goal I can use text evidence to respond to expository text.

Respond to Reading

COLLABORATE Talk about the prompt below. Use your notes and evidence from the text to support your answer.

Why do you think scientists consider red foxes and gray wolves to be members of the same family?

_____

_____

_____

_____

_____

_____

_____

_____

_____

Quick Tip

Use these sentence starters to talk about the wolves and foxes.

Foxes and wolves are members of the same family because . . .

Some things they have in common are . . .

Grammar Connections

The sentence "A rabbit runs away when it sees a predator" is a complex sentence because it has one part that can be a complete sentence ("A rabbit runs away") and another that can't. Try to use complex sentences in your response.

CHECK IN 1 > 2 > 3 > 4

Animal Behaviors

COLLABORATE

Some challenges in animal habitats may be caused by changing seasons. For example, when winter arrives, some animals adapt to colder temperatures by hibernating. Some adapt to warmer temperatures by shedding their coat. With a partner, select an animal to research. Find information and photographs of your animal to create a collage.

Step 1 **Set a Goal** Brainstorm a list of animals you are interested in. Select one to research.

Step 2 **Identify Sources** Ask questions about your animal that you can answer through research. You can ask where your animal lives, what it eats, and how it responds to changing seasons. Find books and reliable websites with relevant, or related, information to answer your questions.

Step 3 **Find and Record Information** Take notes on your sources. Also collect photographs of your animal and its habitat.

Step 4 **Organize and Combine Information** Choose the pieces of information you want to include in your collage. Think of captions you can add to the photographs you found.

Step 5 **Create and Present** Create your collage with your partner by adding facts, photographs, and captions to a poster. You can also include illustrations, maps, and diagrams. Present your collage to the class.

> **Quick Tip**
>
> Remember to use reliable sources. Make sure your facts are correct and can be found in more than one source.

Brian E Kushner/Shutterstock

CHECK IN 1 2 3 4

Amazing Wildlife of the Mojave

 How does the author use words and phrases to help you visualize how the chuckwalla protects itself?

Literature Anthology:
pages 304–315

Talk About It Reread **Literature Anthology** page 307. Talk with a partner about how the chuckwalla protects itself.

Cite Text Evidence What words does the author use to describe what the chuckwalla does to protect itself? Write text evidence in the chart.

Make Inferences

An inference is a conclusion you make based on evidence. Make an inference about how the author feels about how the chuckwalla protects itself. Find evidence to support your inference.

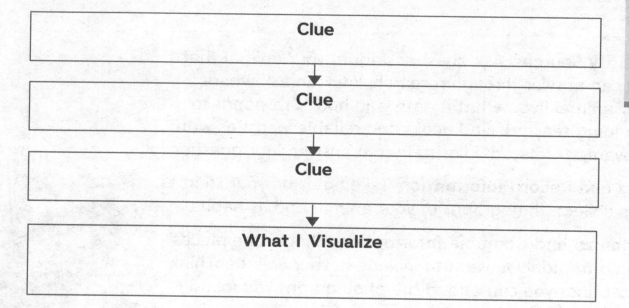

Clue

↓

Clue

↓

Clue

↓

What I Visualize

Write I can visualize how the chuckwalla protects itself because

_____

_____

CHECK IN 1 > 2 > 3 > 4

How does the author help you understand how light-colored and dark-colored animals survive in the desert?

 Talk About It Reread **Literature Anthology** page 309. Talk about how the author structures the text.

Cite Text Evidence What text evidence shows how animals survive in the Mojave Desert? Write it in the chart.

Light-Colored Animals	Dark-Colored Animals

Write The author helps me understand how light-colored and

dark-colored animals survive by _____

_____

_____

_____

CHECK IN ▸ 1 ▸ 2 ▸ 3 ▸ 4

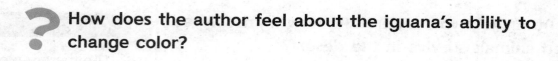

? How does the author feel about the iguana's ability to change color?

Talk About It Reread **Literature Anthology** page 314. Talk with a partner about how the author describes what iguanas do.

Cite Text Evidence What clues help you see how the author feels about what iguanas can do? Write evidence to support your answer.

Text Evidence	How the Author Feels

Write I know how the author feels about iguanas because _____

_____

_____

CHECK IN 1 2 3 4

Respond to Reading

 Talk about the prompt below. Use your notes and evidence from the text to support your answer.

How does the author help you understand how he feels about wildlife in the Mojave?

_____

_____

_____

_____

_____

_____

_____

_____

_____

_____

Quick Tip

Use these sentence starters to talk about how the author feels about wildlife in the Mojave.

The author says that living in the desert is . . .

He tells about how the animals . . .

This helps me know that he feels . . .

CHECK IN ⟩ 1 ⟩ 2 ⟩ 3 ⟩ 4 ⟩

Literature Anthology:
pages 318–319

Little Half Chick

1   Once in Mexico, an unusual chick hatched. He had only one eye, one wing, and one leg. He was named Little Half Chick. He quickly learned to hop faster on one leg than most chickens could walk on two. He was a curious and adventurous chick and soon grew tired of his barnyard environment. One day he decided to hop to Mexico City to meet the mayor.

2   Along the way, he hopped by a stream blocked with weeds. "Could you clear these weeds away so my water can run freely?" the stream gurgled. Little Half Chick helped the stream. Then he hopped on.

3   It started to rain. A small fire on the side of the road crackled, "Please give me shelter from this rain, or I will go out!" Little Half Chick stretched out his wing to protect the fire until the rain stopped.

Reread and use the prompts to take notes in the text.

In the first paragraph, **circle** words and phrases that describe Little Half Chick. Write them here.

_____

_____

_____

COLLABORATE

Reread paragraphs 2 and 3. Talk with a partner about what Little Half Chick does to help the stream and the fire. **Underline** text evidence.

4   Further down the road Little Half Chick met a wind that was tangled in a prickly bush. "Please untangle me," it whispered. Little Half Chick untangled the wind. Then he hopped on to Mexico City.

5   Little Half Chick did not meet the mayor. He met the mayor's cook. She grabbed him, plunged him into a pot of water, and lit a fire. However, the fire and the water remembered Little Half Chick's kindness. The fire refused to burn, and the water refused to boil. Then, the grateful wind picked him up and carried him safely to the top of the highest tower in Mexico City.

6   Little Half Chick became a weather vane. His flat body told everyone below the direction the wind blew. And he learned this lesson: Always help someone in need because you don't know when you'll need help.

Reread paragraph 4. **Circle** how Little Half Chick helps the wind.

COLLABORATE

Reread paragraphs 5 and 6. Talk with a partner about what happens to Little Half Chick when he meets the mayor's cook. **Underline** words and phrases that describe what happens.

How does Little Half Chick escape the pot of water? Make a check mark beside the text evidence. Summarize what happens.

_____

_____

_____

_____

_____

_____

_____

? **What words and phrases help you visualize how Little Half Chick escapes the cook's pot of water?**

Talk About It Reread paragraph 5 on page 173. Turn and talk with a partner about how Little Half Chick escapes.

Cite Text Evidence What words and phrases help you picture what happens? Write text evidence in the chart.

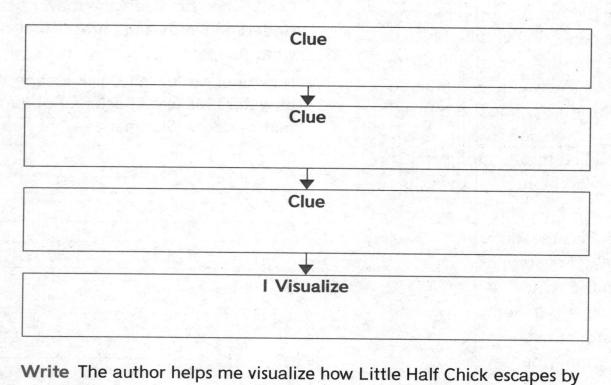

Clue

↓

Clue

↓

Clue

↓

I Visualize

Write The author helps me visualize how Little Half Chick escapes by

_____

_____

_____

CHECK IN 1 2 3 4

Theme

An author often has a theme, or message, that he or she wants the reader to learn from the text. The author uses plot events and details about the characters to develop the theme throughout the story.

🔍 FIND TEXT EVIDENCE

In paragraph 6 of "Little Half Chick" on page 173, the author states the theme of the fable. The events in the story lead up to this lesson that Little Half Chick learns.

> Little Half Chick became a weather vane. His flat body told everyone below the direction the wind blew. And he learned this lesson: Always help someone in need because you don't know when you'll need help.

Your Turn Reread "Little Half Chick" on pages 172 and 173.

- How do the plot events help the author develop the theme?

_____

- What words and phrases in paragraph 5 develop the theme and help you understand the lesson Little Half Chick learns?

_____

Before writing, think about what you want your readers to learn. Write down the theme, or message, you want to share. Then think of details and plot events that you can include to help develop your theme for your readers.

CHECK IN ⟩ 1 ⟩ 2 ⟩ 3 ⟩ 4

How do this photograph, the photographs in *Amazing Wildlife of the Mojave*, and the illustrations in "Little Half Chick" help you understand how animals adapt to challenges?

Talk About It Look at the photograph and read the caption. Talk with a partner about what you see.

Cite Text Evidence Circle the sea cucumber crab. Now **draw a circle** about the same size somewhere on the sea cucumber. Compare what's inside both circles. What do you notice? How is what you learned similar to what you learned from the photographs and illustrations in the texts you read?

Write Photographs and illustrations help

me understand _____

_____

_____

_____

_____

_____

_____

Rene Frederic/Pixtal/age fotostock

Quick Tip

The photograph and caption can help you understand how sea cucumber crabs protect themselves. Use this knowledge to compare the photograph to the texts you read.

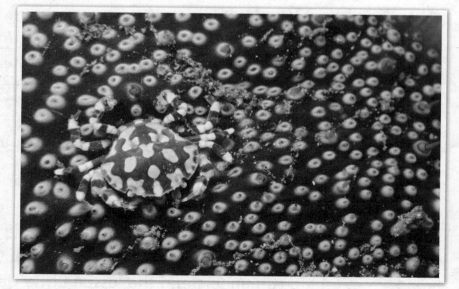

Do you see the sea cucumber crab? He's there. He's resting on a sea cucumber. These crabs use camouflage to protect themselves from animals that want to eat them.

CHECK IN 1 2 3 4

My Goal I know how animals adapt to challenges in their habitat.

Plan a Nature Podcast

Think over what you learned about how animals adapt to challenges in their habitats. Why is it important to learn about animals? Why is it important to protect animals and their habitats?

1 Look at your Build Knowledge notes in your reader's notebook.

2 Plan a podcast, or audio recording, that will help listeners learn more about nature. Choose three or more animals from the texts you read to talk about in your podcast. You can also include other animals you know about.

3 Write a short script for your podcast. Use the animals you selected in Step 2 to help people understand why protecting animals and their habitats is important. Use new vocabulary words you learned.

Think about what you learned in this text set. Fill in the bars on page 155.

Build Knowledge

Essential Question

How can others inspire us?

Build Vocabulary

Write new words you learned about inspiration and the people who inspire us. Draw lines and circles for the words you write.

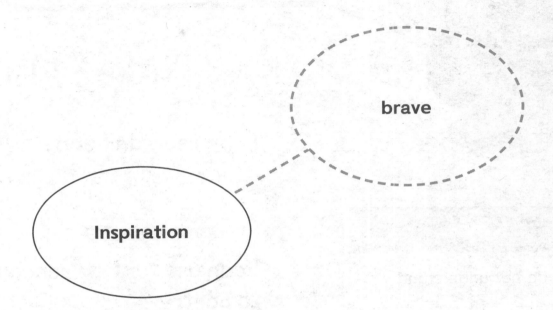

brave

Inspiration

Go online to **my.mheducation.com** and read the "An Inspirational Poet" Blast. Think about why learning about inspirational people who lived long ago is important. Then blast back your response.

Think about what you already know.
Fill in the bars. Let's keep learning!

What I Know Now

I can read and understand poetry.

| 1 | 2 | 3 | 4 |

Key

1 = I do not understand.

2 = I understand but need more practice.

3 = I understand.

4 = I understand and can teach someone.

I can use text evidence to respond to poetry.

| 1 | 2 | 3 | 4 |

I know how others can inspire us.

| 1 | 2 | 3 | 4 |

STOP You will come back to the next page later.

> Think about what you learned. Fill in the bars. Keep working hard!

What I Learned

I can read and understand poetry.

1 2 3 4

I can use text evidence to respond to poetry.

1 2 3 4

I know how others can inspire us.

1 2 3 4

My Goal I can read and understand poetry.

TAKE NOTES

As you read, make note of interesting words and important details.

_____

_____

_____

_____

_____

_____

_____

Ginger's Fingers

Ginger's fingers are shooting stars,
They talk of adventurous trips to Mars.
    Fingers talking without words,
    Signing when sounds can't be heard.

Ginger's fingers are ocean waves,
They talk of fish and deep sea caves.
    Fingers talking without words,
    Signing when sounds can't be heard.

Ginger's fingers are butterflies,
They talk of a honey-gold sunrise.
    Fingers talking without words,
    Signing when sounds can't be heard.

Essential Question

How can others inspire us?

Read about different ways that people inspire others.

The Giant

Dodge, dart, dash,
　　Zigzag, slash!
I sizzle, SIZZLE, when I dribble,
I'm lightning on the court.
My team calls me The Giant,
Even though I'm kinda short.

The other team might laugh to see
A player tiny as a flea.

But I'm a rocket, fiery hot,
Watch me soar, SOAR, on my jump shot!

Stretching, flexing, push, push, PUSH,
My ball flies up and in—Swoosh Woosh!

I show them all
You don't need tall
To rule the ball!

(t)MM Productions/CORBIS; (b)Fuse/Getty Images

FIND TEXT EVIDENCE

Read

Page 182

Rhymed Verse

In the second stanza, **underline** two words that rhyme.

Repetition

Draw a box around the lines that are repeated, or are the same, in all three stanzas.

Page 183

Metaphor

Circle a metaphor in the third stanza. What two things are being compared?

_____

_____

_____

_____

Reread

Author's Craft

Why is "The Giant" a good title for this poem?

FIND TEXT EVIDENCE

Read

Page 184

Metaphor

Underline two metaphors in the first stanza.

Repetition

Draw a box around the repetition in the second stanza. What does it help you visualize?

Theme

How does the crew feel in the third stanza?

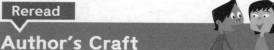

Reread

Author's Craft

How does the poet help you understand how the weather changes in "Captain's Log"?

Captain's Log, May 12, 1868

We set sail from a port in Spain,
Sun high, no sign of rain.
The sea was satin, so blue—so blue.
Our ship was a bird, we flew—we flew.

Just past noon, how very weird,
Came a sound that we most feared.
Thunder rumbled, a giant drum.
Thunder rumbled, rum tum tum.

Rain was pouring, pouring.
The wind was a monster, roaring, roaring.
My crew, extremely terrified,
Froze at their posts, pale and wide-eyed.

A huge wave lifted up our ship,
My feet began to slip, slip, slip.
I knew that it was up to me,
To guide us through that stormy sea.

I grabbed a rope, reached for the mast,
And got back to the helm at last—at last.
Shook off the rain, looked at my crew,
"Steady lads, I'll get us through."

The crew heard my call,
Each lad stood up tall.
All hands now on deck, we trimmed every sail.
Courageous, together, we rode out that gale.

Moon

Crashing waves below,
Thundering dark clouds above.
The full Moon sails through.

Whale

Whale rising for breath,
A short rest from its journey
Across a vast sea.

Make Connections

Which poem do you find most inspiring? Why?

FIND TEXT EVIDENCE

Read

Page 185
Haiku

How many syllables are in each line of "Moon"?

_____

_____

Theme

What do you think is the theme, or main message, of "Whale"?

_____

_____

_____

_____

Reread

Author's Craft

How does the poet who wrote "Moon" help you visualize what is happening in the poem?

Vocabulary

Use the example sentences to talk with a partner about each word. Then answer the questions.

adventurous

You must be **adventurous** to try scuba diving.

What else do you have to be adventurous to try?

_____

_____

courageous

The **courageous** firefighter rescued people from a burning building.

Describe another person who is courageous.

_____

_____

extremely

Cactuses can grow in **extremely** dry places.

Describe a time when you were extremely cold.

_____

_____

weird

The Venus flytrap is a **weird** and strange plant that eats insects.

What is a synonym for _weird_?

_____

_____

Poetry Terms

free verse

Some of Emma's poems are written in **free-verse** rhyme, and some are not.

What rule don't free-verse poems have to follow?

_____

_____

narrative poem

I wrote a **narrative poem** about the American Revolution.

What would you like to write a narrative poem about?

_____

_____

repetition

Repeating words or phrases to create rhythm is called **repetition**.

Name one effect of using repetition.

_____

_____

rhyme

The words *night* and *right* **rhyme** because they end in the same sound.

Write two other words that rhyme.

_____

_____

Build Your Word List Reread the list of interesting words you noted on page 182. Choose a word and look up its definition. In your reader's notebook, write the word and the definition that best fits how the word is used in the poem.

Metaphor

A metaphor compares two different things without using the words *like* or *as*. "His teeth are white pearls" is a metaphor. It compares teeth to pearls. It helps me visualize bright, white teeth.

🔍 FIND TEXT EVIDENCE

On page 182, I read that "Ginger's fingers are shooting stars." This is a metaphor. It compares Ginger's fingers to shooting stars. It helps me picture Ginger's fingers moving quickly.

> Ginger's fingers are shooting stars,
> They talk of adventurous trips to Mars.
> Fingers talking without words,
> Signing when sounds can't be heard.

Your Turn Reread "Ginger's Fingers" on page 182. Find another metaphor. What two things are compared? What does it help you visualize?

_____

_____

CHECK IN 1 ⟩ 2 ⟩ 3 ⟩ 4

Repetition and Rhymed Verse

Repetition means that words or phrases in a poem are repeated. **Rhymed verse** is a form of poetry that uses rhyme. This is when two or more words end with the same sound, as in *pouring* and *roaring*.

FIND TEXT EVIDENCE

Reread the first stanza of "Captain's Log" on page 184. Listen for repeated words or phrases. Think about why the poet uses repetition.

Page 184

Captain's Log, May 12, 1868

We set sail from a port in Spain,
Sun high, no sign of rain.
The sea was satin, so blue—so blue.
Our ship was a bird, we flew—we flew.

Just past noon, how very weird,
Came a sound that we most feared.
Thunder rumbled, a giant drum.
Thunder rumbled, rum tum tum.

Rain was pouring, pouring.
The wind was a monster, roaring, roaring.

In the first stanza, the poet repeats the words so blue *and* we flew. *These words also rhyme. This repetition gives the poem a musical quality. It helps me feel the waves and how the ship moves on the sea.*

Your Turn Reread the rest of "Captain's Log." Find two more examples of repetition and two examples of rhyme. Write them here.

_____

_____

Narrative, Free Verse, and Haiku

Narrative poetry tells a story with a setting and characters. It often rhymes and has stanzas, or groups of lines, of the same length. **Free-verse poetry** doesn't always rhyme. It can have stanzas of different lengths. It can tell a story or express a feeling. **Haikus** use three lines to describe a scene or idea and don't usually rhyme. The first and last lines have five syllables, and the middle line has seven.

Readers to Writers

When writing a poem, select the genre that best fits your purpose. Ask yourself: *Do I want to tell a story or just express a feeling? Would my idea work best with regular stanzas and rhymes, or would it be better as free verse?*

FIND TEXT EVIDENCE

I can tell that "Captain's Log" is a narrative poem. It is a story of a ship's captain who inspires his crew during a bad storm.

Page 184

Captain's Log, May 12, 1868

We set sail from a port in Spain,
Sun high, no sign of rain.
The sea was satin, so blue—so blue.
Our ship was a bird, we flew—we flew.

Just past noon, how very weird,
Came a sound that we most feared.
Thunder rumbled, a giant drum.
Thunder rumbled, rum tum tum.

Rain was pouring, pouring.
The wind was a monster, roaring, roaring.
My crew, extremely terrified,
Froze at their posts, pale and wide-eyed.

A huge wave lifted up our ship,
My feet began to slip, slip, slip.
I knew that it was up to me,
To guide us through that stormy sea.

I grabbed a rope, reached for the mast,
And got back to the helm at last—at last.
Shook off the rain, looked at my crew,
"Steady lads, I'll get us through."

The crew heard my call,
Each lad stood up tall.
All hands now on deck, we trimmed every sail.
Courageous, together, we rode out that gale.

"Captain's Log" is a narrative poem. It rhymes and has stanzas. It's set on a ship during a storm. This setting helps readers understand how characters feel and what they do.

Your Turn Reread "The Giant" on page 183 and "Whale" on page 185. Tell if each is a narrative poem, free-verse poem, or haiku.

_____

_____

_____

CHECK IN 1 2 3 4

Theme

The theme is the main message or lesson in a poem. A poem's topic is what it is about. Paraphrasing the details in a poem can help you figure out the theme and understand how it develops.

🔍 **FIND TEXT EVIDENCE**

All the poems I read are about inspirational people, but each poem has a different theme. I'll reread "The Giant" on page 183 and look for details. I can paraphrase these details to figure out the theme.

Detail
I sizzle when I dribble, and I'm lightning-fast on the basketball court.

↓

Detail
The other team might laugh when they see a player so small.

↓

Theme

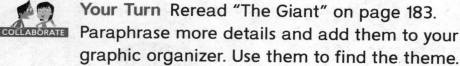 **Your Turn** Reread "The Giant" on page 183. Paraphrase more details and add them to your graphic organizer. Use them to find the theme.

CHECK IN ▷ 1 ▷ 2 ▷ 3 ▷ 4

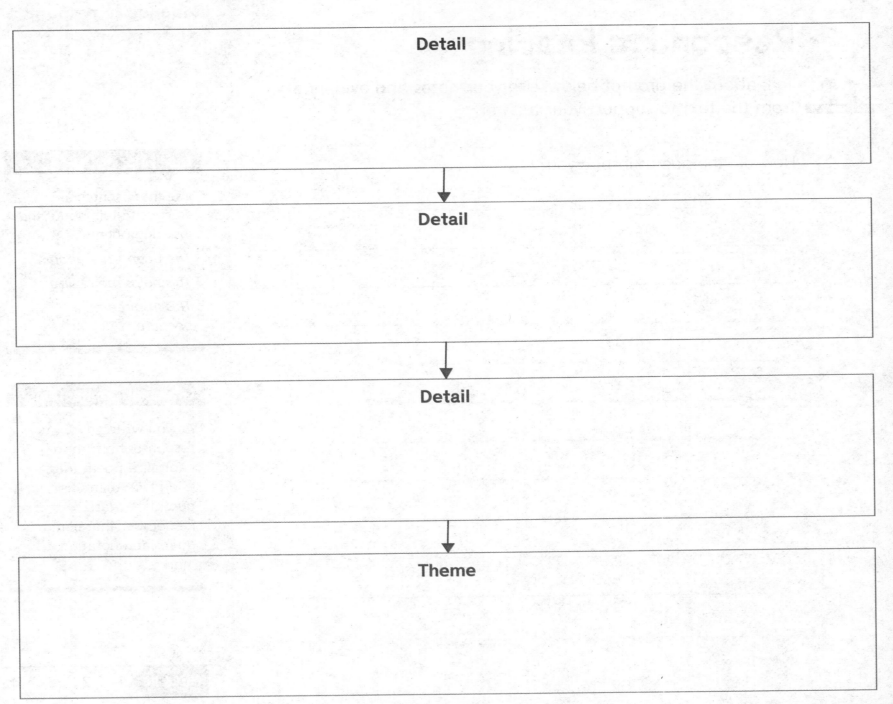

Detail

Detail

Detail

Theme

Respond to Reading

My Goal I can use text evidence to respond to poetry.

COLLABORATE Talk about the prompt below. Use your notes and evidence from the text to support your answer.

How did the poems inspire you?

_____

_____

_____

_____

_____

_____

_____

_____

_____

Quick Tip

Use these sentence starters to talk about the inspiring poems.

The poems are about . . .

This helps me realize . . .

This inspired me because . . .

Grammar Connections

As you write your response, be sure to capitalize poem titles and place them inside quotation marks. Remember that commas go inside quotation marks.

CHECK IN 1 2 3 4

Inspirational Figures

COLLABORATE

Poets often write poems to honor someone who inspires them. Work with a partner and follow the research process to create an acrostic poem about someone who inspires you. In an acrostic poem, the first letters of each line spell a word or name.

Step 1 **Set a Goal** With a partner, discuss some people who inspire you. Choose one person to research.

Step 2 **Identify Sources** Think of questions about your subject that you can answer through research. Look for primary and secondary sources in the library or online.

Step 3 **Find and Record Information** Use your sources to record information that answers your questions. Think about some interesting facts you would like readers of your poem to know.

Step 4 **Organize and Combine Information** Choose the information you want to include in your poem. Start a draft by writing your person's name in a vertical line on a piece of paper.

Step 5 **Create and Present** Finish your acrostic poem by using each letter of your person's name to begin a line that tells something about that person. Use the example as a model. Share your poem with the class and explain why your subject inspires you.

Quick Tip

A primary source is information about a topic created by someone with direct experience. Examples include diaries, letters, and photographs. A secondary source is information created by someone who doesn't have direct knowledge of the topic. Examples include textbooks and encyclopedias.

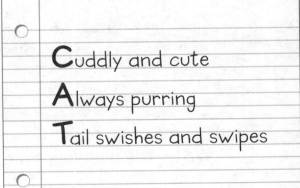

Cuddly and cute

Always purring

Tail swishes and swipes

In this poem, the first letter of each line spells *cat.* Each line describes a cat.

CHECK IN ⟩ 1 ⟩ 2 ⟩ 3 ⟩ 4 ⟩

The Winningest Woman of the Iditarod Dog Sled Race

Literature Anthology: pages 320–321

 ? How does the poet help you understand how the speaker feels about finishing the Iditarod?

 Talk About It Reread **Literature Anthology** page 321. Talk with a partner about what the Iditarod is like.

Cite Text Evidence What words and phrases show how the speaker, or narrator, feels about finishing the race? Write text evidence.

Evaluate Information

Notice that the second line and last line of the poem are the same. How does this repetition help express the speaker's perspective?

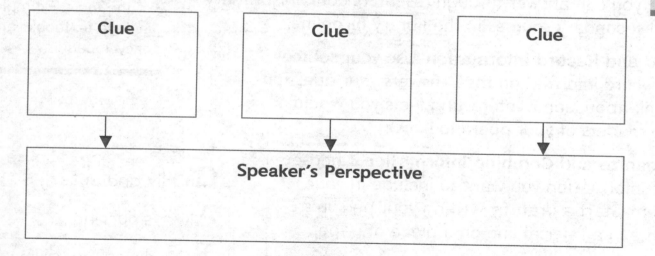

Clue	Clue	Clue

Speaker's Perspective

Write The poet helps me understand how the speaker feels by

_____

_____

CHECK IN 1 2 3 4

The Brave Ones

? How does the use of repetition in "The Brave Ones" help you understand what it is like to fight a fire?

Talk About It Reread **Literature Anthology** page 322. Talk with a partner about how the speaker's words and phrases make you feel.

Cite Text Evidence What words and phrases does the speaker repeat? Add them to the chart. Write what they help you understand.

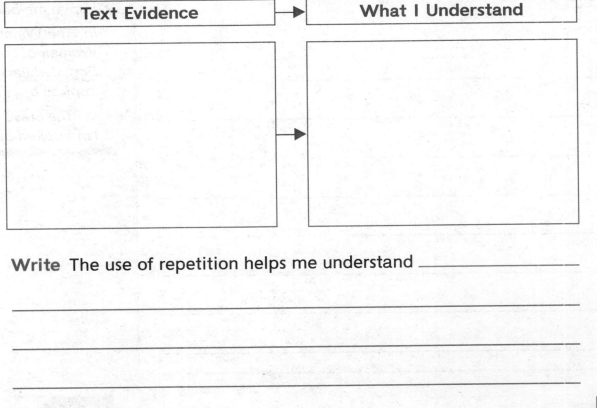

Text Evidence	→	What I Understand

Write The use of repetition helps me understand _____

_____

_____

_____

CHECK IN 1 2 3 4

Respond to Reading

Talk about the prompt below. Use your notes and evidence from the text to support your answer.

How do the people in "The Winningest Woman of the Iditarod Dog Sled Race" and "The Brave Ones" inspire you?

_____

_____

_____

_____

_____

_____

_____

_____

_____

_____

Quick Tip

Use these sentence starters to talk about the poems.

The people in the poems inspire me because . . .

In "The Winningest Woman of the Iditarod Dog Sled Race," I'm inspired by . . .

In "The Brave Ones," I'm inspired by . . .

CHECK IN 1 > 2 > 3 > 4 >

Narcissa

Literature Anthology: pages 324–325

? How do the speaker's words and phrases help you visualize what Narcissa is doing?

Talk About It Reread the first two stanzas on **Literature Anthology** page 325. Talk with a partner about what Narcissa is doing.

Cite Text Evidence What clues in the first and second stanzas help you picture what Narcissa is doing? Write text evidence in the chart.

Quick Tip

A verb is a word that shows action. Look for verbs to help you visualize what characters are doing.

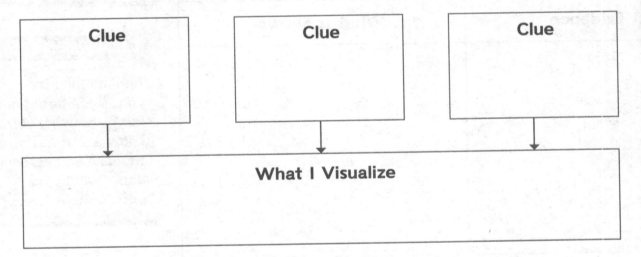

Clue	Clue	Clue

What I Visualize

Write I can visualize what Narcissa is doing because _____

_____

_____

CHECK IN 1 2 3 4

? **Why does the speaker repeat the word *still* at the end of the poem?**

COLLABORATE

Talk About It Reread the third and fourth stanzas on **Literature Anthology** page 325. Talk with a partner about what Narcissa is doing and how she is changing.

Cite Text Evidence What clues help you understand why the speaker repeats the word *still?* Write text evidence in the chart.

Text Evidence	What It Shows

Write The speaker repeats the word *still* to _____

_____

_____

Quick Tip

Use these sentence starters to talk about how the speaker uses repetition.

I read that Narcissa is . . .

The speaker wants me to know that . . .

 Make Inferences

An inference is a conclusion based on facts. Use what you know about Narcissa to make an inference about what kind of person she is.

CHECK IN 1 2 3 4

Imagery

Poets choose words and phrases that help you visualize, or picture in your mind, what is happening in a poem. This is called imagery.

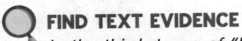 **FIND TEXT EVIDENCE**

*In the third stanza of "Narcissa" on **Literature Anthology** page 325, the speaker says that Narcissa looks like an ancient queen "in pomp and purple veil." This description helps me picture Narcissa sitting tall on her throne with a purple veil draped over her head.*

 Your Turn Reread "Narcissa" on page 325.

- What is another interesting word or phrase in the poem?

  _____

  _____

  _____

- What does it help you visualize and understand about Narcissa?

  _____

  _____

  _____

Readers to Writers

As you write, use descriptions of how things look, sound, smell, and feel to help your readers picture what is happening and what characters are experiencing.

? How is the man in the photograph below like the characters in "The Winningest Woman of the Iditarod Dog Sled Race," "The Brave Ones," and "Narcissa"?

Talk About It Look at the photograph and read the caption. Discuss what the grandfather and his grandson are doing.

Cite Text Evidence Circle details in the photograph that help you understand what each person is doing. **Underline** evidence in the caption that gives you more information about what is going on.

Write The grandfather and the characters in the poems are alike

because they _____

_____

_____

_____

_____

_____

_____

Alex is a gardener. He works in a community garden on the weekends. He loves to take his grandson with him to show him how to grow vegetables and flowers.

CHECK IN 1 2 3 4

Design an Inspirational Poster

Think over what you learned about how others can inspire us. What are some people or things that inspire you? How can inspiration help you do or create something new?

1. Look at your Build Knowledge notes in your reader's notebook.

2. Use the texts you read to think of a message that can inspire others. Then think of a design for an inspirational poster that can include your message. Plan how you can arrange illustrations and text on your poster.

3. Create your final poster. On the back, write a short paragraph that explains how inspirational people and ideas can help us create or do something new. Use evidence from the poems you read to support your ideas. Also include new vocabulary words you learned.

Think about what you learned in this text set. Fill in the bars on page 181.

Think about what you already know. Fill in the bars. It's important to keep learning.

Key

1 = I do not understand.

2 = I understand but need more practice.

3 = I understand.

4 = I understand and can teach someone.

What I Know Now

I can write an expository essay.

| 1 | 2 | 3 | 4 |

I can synthesize information from three sources.

| 1 | 2 | 3 | 4 |

STOP You will come back to the next page later.

What I Learned

I can write an expository essay.

I can synthesize information from three sources.

1 2 3 4

WRITE TO SOURCES

You will answer an expository writing prompt using sources and a rubric.

ANALYZE THE RUBRIC

A rubric tells you what needs to be included in your writing.

Purpose, Focus, and Organization

Read the second bullet. What is a central idea?

_____

_____

Read the fifth bullet. What are two things your essay must include?

_____

_____

Evidence and Elaboration

Underline the words in the fourth bullet that tell you how to elaborate on your topic.

Expository Writing Rubric

Purpose, Focus, and Organization • Score 4

- Stays focused on the purpose, audience, and task
- **States the central idea in a clear way**
- Uses transitional strategies, such as the use of signal, or linking, words and phrases, to show how ideas are connected
- Has a logical progression of ideas
- Begins with a strong introduction and ends with a conclusion

Evidence and Elaboration • Score 4

- Supports the central idea with convincing details
- Relevant evidence is integrated smoothly and thoroughly
- Has strong examples of relevant evidence, or supporting details, with references to multiple sources
- Uses elaborative techniques, such as examples, definitions, and quotations from sources
- Uses precise language to express ideas clearly
- Uses appropriate academic and domain-specific language that matches the audience and purpose of the essay
- Uses different sentence types and lengths

Turn to page 240 for the complete Expository Writing Rubric.

Central Idea

Stating the Central Idea A strong expository essay has a clearly stated central idea. Read the paragraph below. The central idea is highlighted.

> Would you buy a machine that allows you to see with your tongue? Even if it costs a thousand dollars? Some people may not be interested. But if you experience vision loss, you might say yes. **Inventors are creating new devices to help people with disabilities.** A machine that allows you to see with your tongue is one example of such a device. I have always enjoyed learning about inventors and the things they create.

What does the central idea tell you about the focus of the essay?

_____

_____

Relevant Details Writers use relevant details as evidence to develop and support their central idea. Details should strongly support the stated central idea. Strong writers do not include unimportant details in their writing.

Read the paragraph above. **Cross out** an unimportant detail that does not support the central idea.

Writers have an audience in mind when they write. They make choices about what to include based on their audience. Reread the paragraph about how inventors are using technology to help people. Who is the audience?

ANALYZE THE STUDENT MODEL

Paragraph 1

Write a detail from Mina's introduction that caught your attention.

_____

_____

_____

Read the first paragraph of Mina's essay. The central idea is highlighted.

Paragraph 2

What is an example of relevant evidence that Mina uses to support her central idea?

_____

_____

Circle the phrase that tells how this invention is helping people with disabilities.

Student Model: Expository Text

Mina responded to the writing prompt: _Write an expository essay about inventors who use technology to help people with disabilities._ Read Mina's essay below.

1   What if you could watch a baseball game with your tongue? Or feel a song on your skin? Someday it might be possible, thanks to new inventions. These inventions could be very important for people who have vision or hearing loss. Inventors are making new devices to help people with disabilities.

2   The first source describes an invention that helps people with vision loss see with their tongues. The invention uses special glasses with a camera, as well as a device that goes in your mouth. The glasses send information about what they see to the device. This creates a signal on your tongue, and that signal travels to your brain. The signal allows your brain to see shapes and colors. This can allow people with vision loss to see the objects that surround them.

3   The second source describes inventions that make it easier for people with vision loss to use technology. For example, a new kind of tablet lets people use braille. Braille is usually raised bumps on paper. Braille lets people with loss of vision read with their fingers. Touch screens are usually smooth, but an inventor

found a way to add braille to a touch screen. Inventors have also created a smart phone with a similar technology. These inventions are very useful because they provide people with vision loss more options for using modern technology and communicating with others.

4   Inventors are also helping people with hearing loss. Scientists are working on using other senses to get information about sound to the brain. For example, there is a special vest that is full of microphones that pick up sounds. The sounds make vibrations. If you wear the vest, you can feel the vibrations on your skin. This creates a signal that your skin can send to your brain. As a result, the vest allows people to hear in a new way.

5   These are some of the ways inventors are using technology to help others. People with vision loss can use special glasses to see with their tongues. They can also use new kinds of touch screens and smart phones. People with hearing loss can use a new vest that lets them feel sounds. These inventions can be a great help to people with disabilities.

Paragraph 3

Reread the third paragraph. **Underline** examples of elaboration that Mina uses. What important detail does this elaboration support?

_____

_____

Paragraph 4

What is an example of a signal, or linking, word or phrase Mina uses to connect her ideas?

_____

_____

Reread the conclusion. **Underline** the idea that Mina repeats from paragraph 1.

Apply the Rubric

With a partner, use the rubric on page 204 to discuss why Mina scored a 4 on her essay.

(bkgd)Titus Group/Shutterstock, (paperclips)Oleksandr Derevianko/Shutterstock, (tr)Fat Camera/iStock/Getty Images

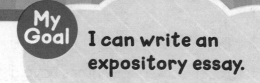

Analyze the Prompt

Writing Prompt

Write an expository essay to explain to your class how the special abilities and qualities of animals are being used to help people.

Purpose, Audience, and Task Reread the writing prompt. What is your purpose for writing? My purpose is to _____

_____

Who will your audience be? My audience will be _____

_____

What type of writing is the prompt asking for? _____

_____

Set a Purpose for Reading Sources Asking questions about what special abilities and qualities animals have will help you figure out your purpose for reading. It also helps you understand what you already know about the topic. Before you read the passage set about animals helping humans, write a question here.

_____

_____

_____

Read the following passage set.

"Woof!" Rrrread to Me, Please?

1   Scooter and Molly wait patiently in a corner of the library. They are not reading. They don't have library cards. They don't even know what a book is. Scooter and Molly are special dogs called therapy animals. Their job is to listen. They have been trained for the job.

2   These dogs are participants at the Wadleigh Memorial Library in New Hampshire in a program called Paws to Read. Though it's a busy day at the library, these dogs don't bark or run around. They come here to sit quietly while kids read to them. **Reading to dogs makes reading more enjoyable.** "The children always have smiles on their faces," says Bill Dahlkamp from Support Dogs, Inc.

3   Why do kids read books to dogs? For those struggling with reading, or for kids who just like to read aloud, reading to a dog is fun. And unlike other kids, dogs never giggle if you mispronounce a word.

4   One volunteer who brings her dog to the library explains. There is a lot less pressure reading to a dog. Dogs are completely accepting. "Even three-year-olds get interested in reading to a dog."

5   The dogs at this library today seem interested in the kids, especially Scooter. Scooter is a long-haired Chihuahua. **A girl strokes Scooter's fur. Scooter sits patiently as the girl sounds out some words.**

EXPOSITORY ESSAY

FIND TEXT EVIDENCE 🔍

Paragraph 1
Read paragraph 1. Who are Scooter and Molly?

_____

Paragraph 2
Read the highlighted central idea in paragraph 2. **Draw a box around** a detail that supports it.

Paragraphs 3–4
Underline ways that reading to a dog is helpful. Summarize them.

_____

_____

Paragraph 5
Read the highlighted details in paragraph 5. How do these details support the central idea?

_____

_____

📝 **Take Notes** Summarize the central idea and give examples of relevant details.

FIND TEXT EVIDENCE

Paragraph 6

Read the highlighted central idea in paragraph 6.

Paragraph 7

Read the highlighted detail in paragraph 7. How does this detail support the central idea?

_____

_____

_____

Paragraph 8

Underline the special ability of parrots.

Paragraphs 9–10

There are many benefits to caring for a parrot. Write three.

_____

_____

_____

Take Notes Summarize the central idea and give details that support that idea.

SOURCE 2

Parrot Pals

6   Most support animals are dogs. But did you know that birds can be support animals too? **A program in Washington state matches parrots and people, helping them both at the same time.**

7   **The parrots need someone to take care of them.** The program places them with veterans, or people who were soldiers. Some of the veterans have something called PTSD. PTSD is Posttraumatic Stress Disorder, and this can affect thoughts, feelings, and actions. Veterans with PTSD may have trouble relaxing. PTSD can make it hard to be around other people.

8   This is where the parrots can help. Parrots are smart animals. Like dogs, they are friendly. They enjoy being with people. Unlike dogs, they can often be trained to talk! Parrots do not speak in the same way that humans do. However, they may repeat words that they hear a lot.

9   If a parrot gets to know you, the bird might hop onto your shoulder. Your parrot might like to sing and dance with you. What a great friend a parrot can make!

10   Parrots can give a lot to veterans. Caring for the parrots gives them something interesting to do. This can help a veteran relax. Some veterans say that having a parrot helped them talk to people again. When parrots and people help each other, everybody wins!

A Dog's SUPER POWER

SOURCE 3

11   Dogs are great at smelling things. It's their super power! **Some dogs use their super power to help people.** They are trained to be detection dogs. Now conservation groups are training dogs to protect the planet.

12   Conservation detection dogs sniff out invasive species. For example, Santa Cruz Island in California had an invasive ant species. The ants were chasing away important native insects. A conservation group removed the invading ants. To make sure the ants were completely gone, they brought in Tobias. Tobias is a Labrador retriever trained to smell these ants. Tobias sniffed the whole island. Finally, every ant was gone.

13   Detection dogs can also find animal species that are endangered. In Oregon, detection dogs are helping western pond turtles. The turtles are hard to find. Dogs are trained to sniff out the nests. Then a conservation group will guard the eggs.

14   Dogs have used their keen noses to help whales, rhinos, and other animals. Their reward? A treat! A small price for protecting planet Earth.

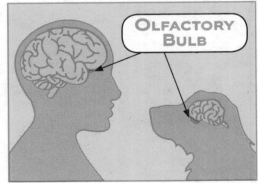

OLFACTORY BULB

The olfactory bulb is where smells are analyzed in the brain.

EXPOSITORY ESSAY

FIND TEXT EVIDENCE 🔍

Paragraphs 11–12
Read the highlighted central idea in paragraph 11.

Underline text evidence in paragraph 12 that supports the central idea.

Paragraphs 13–14
What is another way dogs help people and the environment?

_____

_____

Diagram
Compare parts of the dog and human brain that are colored in red. Explain what this tells us about a dog's sense of smell.

_____

_____

_____

📝 **Take Notes** Summarize the central idea. Give details that support that idea.

My Goal **I can synthesize information from three sources.**

TAKE NOTES

Read the writing prompt below. Use the three sources, your notes, and the graphic organizer to plan a response.

Writing Prompt *Write an expository essay to explain to your class how the special abilities and qualities of animals are being used to help people.*

Synthesize Information

Review the evidence recorded from each source. How does the information show how animals can use their abilities to help people?

Plan: Organize Ideas

Central Idea	Supporting Ideas
Sometimes the best way to solve a human problem is to use an animal for help.	Animals have special abilities and qualities.

Valentain Jevee/Shutterstock

Relevant Evidence

Source 1	Source 2	Source 3
Dogs can be patient, gentle, and good listeners.		

Draft: Strong Introduction

Strong Openings Use a strong opening to introduce your topic. One way to introduce your topic is to use questions or surprising facts to grab the reader's attention. A strong opening states the topic in a way that makes the reader want to keep reading.

Reread the opening paragraph of Mina's essay about inventors helping people with disabilities. Talk with a partner about how Mina grabs your attention. Then use text evidence to answer the question.

> What if you could watch a baseball game with your tongue? Or feel a song on your skin? Someday it might be possible, thanks to new inventions. These inventions could be very important for people who have vision or hearing loss. Inventors are making new devices to help people with disabilities.

How does Mina make you want to keep reading?

_____

_____

Draft Use your graphic organizer and the example above to write your draft in your writer's notebook. Before you start writing, review the rubric on page 204. Start with a strong introduction and include details to support your central idea.

uniquely india/Getty Images

CHECK IN 1 > 2 > 3 > 4

Revise: Peer Conferences

Review a Draft Listen actively to your partner. Take notes about what you liked and what was difficult to follow. Begin by telling what you liked. Use these sentence starters.

I think your introduction . . .

I like the evidence that supports the central idea because . . .

What did you mean by . . .

After you finish giving each other feedback, reflect on the peer conference. What suggestion was the most helpful?

✔ **Revising Checklist**

☐ Do I have a strong central idea?

☐ Do I have enough relevant evidence to support my central idea?

☐ Do I use signal, or linking, words to show connections between my ideas?

☐ Do I have a strong introduction?

Revision Use the Revising Checklist to help you figure out what text you need to move, elaborate on, or delete. After you finish writing your final draft, use the rubric on pages 240–243 to score your essay.

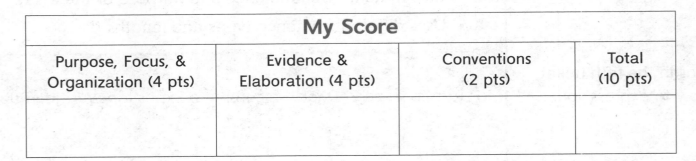

Next, you'll write an expository essay on a new topic.

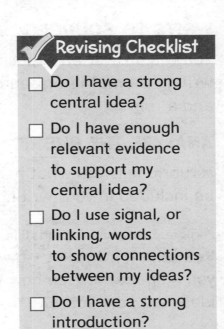

My Score			
Purpose, Focus, & Organization (4 pts)	Evidence & Elaboration (4 pts)	Conventions (2 pts)	Total (10 pts)

WRITE TO SOURCES

You will answer an expository writing prompt using sources and a rubric.

ANALYZE THE RUBRIC

A rubric tells you what needs to be included in your writing.

Purpose, Focus, and Organization

Read the third bullet. How can you help readers see how your ideas are connected?

_____

_____

Evidence and Elaboration

Read the third bullet. What is important to remember when adding evidence to your writing?

_____

_____

Underline words in the fifth bullet that tell you how to express your ideas clearly.

Expository Writing Rubric

Purpose, Focus, and Organization • Score 4

- Stays focused on the purpose, audience, and task
- States the central idea in a clear way
- Uses transitional strategies, such as the use of signal, or linking, words and phrases, to show how ideas are connected
- Has a logical progression of ideas
- Begins with a strong introduction and ends with a conclusion

Evidence and Elaboration • Score 4

- Supports the central idea with convincing details
- Relevant evidence is integrated smoothly and thoroughly
- **Has strong examples of relevant evidence, or supporting details, with references to multiple sources**
- Uses elaborative techniques, such as examples, definitions, and quotations from sources
- Uses precise language to express ideas clearly
- Uses appropriate academic and domain-specific language that matches the audience and purpose of the essay
- Uses different sentence types and lengths

Turn to page 240 for the complete Expository Writing Rubric.

Valentain Jevee/Shutterstock

Relevant Evidence

Use Relevant Evidence A strong expository essay has relevant evidence, or facts, that develops and supports the central idea. Writers can use definitions, quotations, and examples to elaborate on their evidence and grab the reader's attention. Read the paragraph below. The central idea of the paragraph is highlighted.

> Kerry Pakucko is a paramedic in Chicago. She loves her job because she gets to help people. Often, Kerry uses her bicycle to respond to patients. "On the bikes, we can zip through the crowd and get to the patient way faster than an ambulance could," Kerry said in an interview. **This shows how paramedics like Kerry work hard by going as fast as they can to reach people who are in need of help.**

Underline an example of relevant evidence. How does it support the central idea of the paragraph?

_____

Reference Sources When writers use evidence from a source, they reference that source in their writing. This lets readers know where the evidence comes from and gives credit to the source.

Reread the paragraph. Notice the relevant evidence you underlined. Write the source, or where the evidence came from.

Audience and Purpose

When you write an expository essay, you are teaching your audience something you think they should know about your topic. As you write, ask yourself: *What are the most important facts I want to tell my audience? What relevant evidence would help them understand the topic better?*

ANALYZE THE STUDENT MODEL

Paragraph 1

What does Liam do to start his essay in an interesting way?

_____

_____

Read the first paragraph. **Underline** the central idea in Liam's introduction.

Paragraph 2

Read paragraph 2. The central idea of the paragraph is highlighted. One piece of relevant evidence is underlined. How does this support the paragraph's central idea?

_____

_____

Circle three things paramedics must learn to do.

Student Model: Expository Essay

Liam responded to the writing prompt: *Write an expository essay for your school newspaper about how paramedics help the people in their communities.* Read Liam's essay below.

1   What happens when someone calls 9-1-1? He or she connects with a 9-1-1 dispatcher and asks for help. If there is a medical emergency, paramedics are called. Within minutes, an ambulance appears and paramedics jump out. They push a stretcher and carry medical bags filled with special equipment. They rush to help and are trained to know what to do. They help sick and injured patients and make sure they get to the hospital safely. Paramedics are real-life heroes who work hard and use what they know to save lives.

2   According to "The Power of Paramedics," many paramedics go to school for two years to learn how to take care of sick or injured people. There is so much to learn. Paramedics must learn how to respond to emergency calls, check a person's condition, and figure out what to do to help. They study and work hard so that they can help people in their communities.

3   Most of what a paramedic needs is packed into an ambulance. The article "What Is an Ambulance?" describes an ambulance as "an emergency room on wheels." It has lots of

medical equipment. The flashing lights and siren help the ambulance get to the hospital quickly. It has a radio telephone so that the paramedic can talk to doctors at the hospital before they get there. Paramedics know how to use everything in their ambulance. This helps them save lives.

4   Kerry Pakucko is a paramedic in Chicago. She loves her job because she gets to help people. Often, Kerry uses her bicycle to respond to patients. "On the bikes, we can zip through the crowd and get to the patient way faster than an ambulance could," Kerry said in an interview. This shows how paramedics like Kerry work hard by going as fast as they can to reach people who are in need of help.

5   When there is an emergency and 9-1-1 is called, paramedics are on the scene to help. They calm patients down, get important information, and bring sick or injured people to the emergency room. Their training and experience helps save lives.

(bkgd)Titus Group/Shutterstock, (paperclips)Oleksandr Derevianko/Shutterstock, (tr)Radius Images/Image Source

EXPOSITORY ESSAY

Paragraph 3

Read the third paragraph. Underline relevant evidence. How does this evidence support the central idea in the introduction?

_____

_____

_____

Paragraph 4

What elaborative technique does Liam use in paragraph 4?

_____

_____

_____

Paragraph 5

Read the conclusion. Underline the detail that Liam repeats from paragraph 1.

Apply the Rubric

With a partner, use the rubric on page 216 to discuss why Liam's essay was successful.

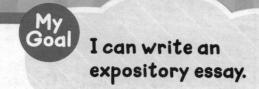

Analyze the Prompt

Writing Prompt

Write an expository essay for a career fair at school. Explain why it is important for firefighters to have certain traits and skills to do their job.

Purpose, Audience, and Task Reread the writing prompt. What is your purpose for writing? My purpose is to _____

_____

Who will your audience be? My audience will be _____

_____

What type of writing is the prompt asking for? _____

_____

Set a Purpose for Reading Sources Asking questions about what firefighters do will help you figure out your purpose for reading. It also helps you understand what you already know about the topic. Before you read the passage set about firefighters, write a question here.

_____

_____

_____

Read the following passage set.

A Tough Two Minutes

1   Every year, firefighters from around the world compete in fitness challenges. They are often called "the toughest two minutes in sports." **These contests highlight the strength and speed firefighters need to do their jobs.**

2   Firefighters participate by completing an obstacle course. They are dressed in PPE. This stands for Personal Protective Equipment. Firefighters wear PPE when responding to an emergency. It includes a fire-resistant suit, helmet, breathing mask, and air tank. Altogether, it weighs over forty-five pounds!

3   The course starts with a five-story stair climb. At the top of the stairs, a forty-pound sack is pulled up from the ground. After racing back down the stairs, competitors use a heavy hammer to move a weight. Then they run and pull a heavy fire hose. Finally, they drag a 175-pound mannequin across the finish line. All this is done in under two minutes! Competitors must be in excellent shape to complete the challenge.

4   The course mimics real situations firefighters face. A real fire can spread through an entire home in less than five minutes. So, like competitors in a fitness challenge, firefighters on the job must be swift and strong.

Adam Berry/Stringer/Getty Images News/Getty Images

EXPOSITORY ESSAY

FIND TEXT EVIDENCE

Paragraphs 1–2
Read the highlighted central idea. What relevant evidence in paragraph 2 develops and supports this central idea?

_____

_____

Paragraphs 3–4
How would dragging a 175-pound mannequin mimic a real situation a firefighter might face?

_____

_____

Underline the sentence that restates the central idea from the introduction in a different way.

Take Notes Paraphrase the central idea of the source. Summarize the relevant evidence that supports it.

FIND TEXT EVIDENCE

Paragraphs 5–6

Underline why it is important for firefighters to study different types of fires.

Paragraph 7

Why do firefighters train in a "burn building"?

_____

_____

_____

Paragraph 8

How do thermal cameras help firefighters do their job?

_____

_____

_____

Take Notes Write one or two quotes from the interview to include in your expository essay.

"Learning the Job: An Interview with Firefighter Grant" by Abigail Fitzwild, Appleseeds, November 1, 2006 © by Carus Publishing Company. Reproduced with permission. All Cricket Media material is copyrighted by Carus Publishing Company, d/b/a Cricket Media, and/or various authors and illustrators. Any commercial use or distribution of material without permission is strictly prohibited. Please visit http://www.cricketmedia.com/info/licensing and http://www.cricketmedia.com/info/licensing2 for licensing and http://www.cricketmedia.com for subscriptions. Art: Anatolir/Shutterstock.

SOURCE 2

AN INTERVIEW WITH
Firefighter Grant

5 Lieutenant Warren Grant is a firefighter. He answered some questions about how courageous firefighters train for their difficult and dangerous jobs.

How did you train to become a firefighter?

6 I completed eleven weeks of training at a firefighting academy. We learned about fire safety. We studied different types of fires, how they start, and how they behave. This helps us better understand how to fight them. We learned to use the equipment. Practicing rope and ladder rescues was another big part of our training.

Is it true that you practice with real fires?

7 Oh yes. We need to know how to manage fires in the real world. In training, we worked in a three-story "burn building." It's built especially for firefighter training. The fires we put out were burning wood and hay. The hay makes a real yellow, smoky fire.

After the academy, is your training over?

8 No. Whenever we get new equipment, for example our thermal camera, we need to learn how to use it. Smoke makes it hard to find people. With the thermal camera, we can see people with the heat their bodies give off. We can find and rescue them much faster.

Thanks, Firefighter Grant, for everything you do!

A Firefighter's Duties

SOURCE 3

9 Firefighters protect life, property, and the environment. To fulfill these duties, they use their training to assess emergency situations and act quickly.

10 **A good fire company, or team of firefighters, works together.** Some may enter a burning building to search for trapped people. Others manage the blaze from outside. They need to stay in contact. If the fire changes, it could affect their action plan. Without teamwork and communication, things could get out of control.

11 Not all emergencies involve fires. Firefighters are also called to help those who are in need of rescue. They help during and after natural disasters. Many firefighters receive paramedic training because of this.

12 Even when there is no emergency, firefighters have work to do. They maintain their equipment. Practice drills keep them ready. Firefighters stay hard at work.

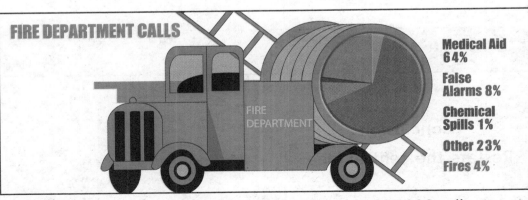

FIRE DEPARTMENT CALLS

Medical Aid 64%
False Alarms 8%
Chemical Spills 1%
Other 23%
Fires 4%

In 2016, fire departments across the U.S. received 35,325,000 calls. Firefighters were called for medical aid more than any other reason.

EXPOSITORY ESSAY

FIND TEXT EVIDENCE

Paragraphs 9–10
Reread paragraph 10. The central idea of the paragraph has been highlighted.

Underline how the writer elaborates on the central idea.

Paragraphs 11–12
What other emergencies do fire companies respond to?

Pie Chart
How does this chart help explain why firefighters receive paramedic training?

 Take Notes Paraphrase the central idea. Summarize relevant evidence that develops and supports it.

(t)mStudioVector/Shutterstock, (b)fortuna82/Shutterstock

WRITING

TAKE NOTES

Read the writing prompt below. Use the three sources, your notes, and the graphic organizer to plan your essay.

Writing Prompt *Write an expository essay for a career fair at school. Explain why it is important for firefighters to have certain traits and skills to do their job.*

Synthesize Information

Think about what you know about firefighters. How do details from the sources and your own knowledge about firefighters help you support the central idea? Discuss your ideas with a partner.

Plan: Organize Ideas

Introduction State the central idea.	Firefighters must be hardworking, brave, and willing to learn new things to do their job quickly and safely.
Body Supporting Ideas	Firefighters must learn to use different kinds of equipment.
Conclusion Restate the central idea.	

Valentain Jevee/Shutterstock

Relevant Evidence		
Source 1	**Source 2**	**Source 3**
Firefighters must know how to use PPE, including a breathing mask and air tank.	Firefighters may need to use thermal cameras in smoky buildings.	

Valentain Jevee/Shutterstock

Draft: Strong Conclusion

Restate the Central Idea An expository essay needs a strong conclusion that stresses its most important points. The conclusion should repeat the central idea of the essay in a new way. Readers should come away from an essay feeling satisfied that the conclusion comes full circle and brings them back to the ideas in the introduction.

Reread "A Tough Two Minutes" on page 221. Notice how the writer restates the central idea in the last paragraph. Rewrite the conclusion paragraph in your own words, restating the central idea in a different way.

_____

_____

_____

_____

 Draft Use your graphic organizer and notes to write your draft in your writer's notebook. Before you start writing, review the rubric on page 216. Remember to restate the central idea in your conclusion paragraph.

CHECK IN 1 2 3 4

Revise: Peer Conferences

COLLABORATE

Review a Draft Listen carefully as your partner reads his or her draft aloud. Say what you like about the draft. Use these sentence starters to discuss your partner's draft.

This supporting idea is strong because . . .

I have a question about . . .

You can make your conclusion stronger by . . .

After you take turns giving each other feedback, write one of the suggestions you will use in your revision.

✔ **Revising Checklist**

☐ Is the central idea clearly stated in the introduction?

☐ Does my evidence strongly support the central idea?

☐ Did I reference sources in my essay?

☐ Do I have a strong conclusion?

☐ Did I check my spelling and punctuation?

Revision After you finish your conference, use the Revising Checklist to figure out what you can change to make your essay better. After you finish your final draft, use the full rubric on pages 240–243 to score your essay.

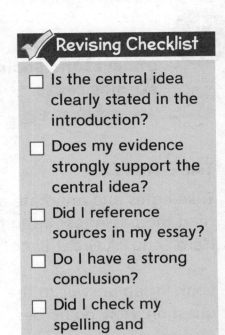

Turn to page 203. Fill in the bars to show what you learned.

My Score

Purpose, Focus, & Organization (4 pts)	Evidence & Elaboration (4 pts)	Conventions (2 pts)	Total (10 pts)

TAKE NOTES

Take notes and annotate as you read the passages "Balto the Hero" and "A Great Race."

Look for an answer to the question. *How do heroes inspire us?*

_____

_____

_____

_____

_____

_____

_____

_____

PASSAGE 1   EXPOSITORY TEXT

BALTO THE HERO

In January 1925, children in Nome, Alaska, were in danger. A deadly illness called diphtheria was making them sick. The medicine that could save them was far away. Airplanes could not get there. It was a big problem. There was no time to lose.

People looked for an answer. They decided to use dogsleds. Dogsleds are a traditional form of transportation. Different dogsled teams carried the medicine in a relay race. Each team was led by a musher, or dogsled driver. Each team carried the medicine part of the way. They raced through a total of 647 miles of snow and ice. It took five and a half days for twenty mushers and about 150 dogs to reach Nome with the medicine.

The mushers and their dogs became instant heroes. The most famous dog was Balto. Balto was the lead sled dog on the last leg of the journey. His team carried the medicine into Nome. Balto became a symbol of the brave mushers and dogs who raced to deliver the medicine.

Balto is still honored today as a canine hero. A statue of Balto stands in Central Park in New York City. The Balto statue attracts many visitors each year.

Balto became a canine celebrity in 1925.

ASSOCIATED PRESS

PASSAGE **2**

EXPOSITORY TEXT

A Great Race

The Iditarod Trail Sled Dog Race is called "The Last Great Race on Earth." When you learn about this race, you will know why. The race happens in Alaska every March. It starts in Anchorage. The finish line is in Nome. That is about 1,000 miles away.

Men and women from all over the world compete. They are called mushers. Each musher leads a dogsled team on a wild, snowy adventure. A dogsled team includes sixteen sled dogs. The dogs are usually Alaskan huskies.

The race honors a historic trail. Long ago, the Iditarod Trail connected places in Alaska that were hard to reach. People traveled along the trail by dogsled. The trail connected towns, villages, and gold-mining camps. In 1925, mushers raced along the trail with medicine to stop a terrible disease.

People have used dogsleds to travel in snowy areas for thousands of years.

Alaska Photography/Moment/Getty Images

TAKE NOTES

After snowmobiles became popular, things changed. People no longer needed dogsleds for winter travel. They didn't need Alaskan huskies to pull sleds. As a result, the dogs were starting to disappear. The Iditarod race was created to preserve the tradition of dogsleds.

The race lasts about eight to fifteen days. The winner gets a cash prize, along with the pride of winning. But another prize goes to the very last musher to cross the finish line. The last-place musher gets the Red Lantern Award. Do you know why? Perseverance is also an important part of the spirit of Alaska!

Huskies are traditionally used as sled dogs.

COMPARE THE PASSAGES

Review your notes on "Balto the Hero" and "A Great Race." Then create a Venn diagram like the one below. Use your notes and diagram to show how information in the two passages is alike and different.

Alike

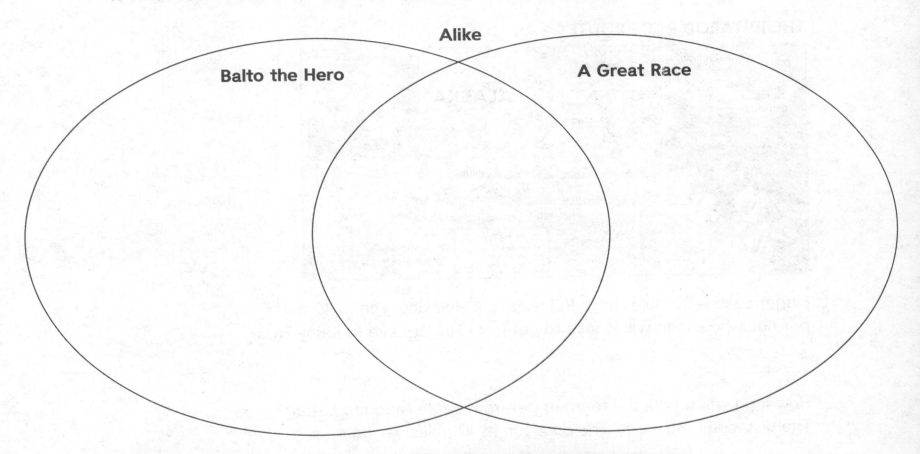

Balto the Hero

A Great Race

Synthesize Information

Think about what you learned from both texts. What do the texts tell you about how we can honor and show our thanks for the heroes who inspire us?

CHECK IN 1 2 3 4

READ A MAP

Maps can help us understand where the places we read about and want to know more about are located. This map shows the route of the Iditarod Trail. Use the map to answer the questions below.

THE IDITAROD RACE ROUTE

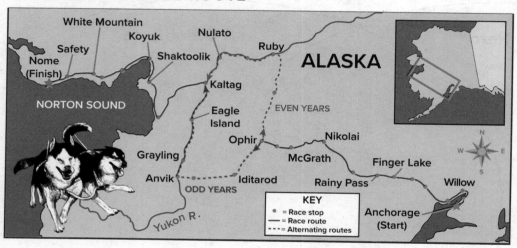

Finger Lake is 30 miles from Rainy Pass. If sled dogs run at 10 miles per hour, how long will it take to get from Finger Lake to Rainy Pass?

_____

How long will it take the team to get from Eagle Island to Kaltag? The distance is 60 miles. The dogs run at 10 miles per hour.

_____

A sled dog team has 16 dogs. Each dog eats one pound of dog food every day. How much dog food will they need for a 10-day race?

_____

WRITE ABOUT AN ANIMAL HERO

Think about the heroic huskies of the Iditarod Trail. One of them, Balto, has a statue in New York City. Think of a special animal you know about.

Why is this animal special? What would a monument to that animal look like?

Write a paragraph in your writer's notebook to explain. Fill out a chart like the one below to organize your writing.

Name of Animal	Type of Animal	What It Looks Like	Why It Is Special	Ideas for a Monument
Merle	Blue Heeler dog	Weighs 40 pounds, has black and gray fur, and has a chewed-up ear	Chases away coyotes	Merle standing on guard, watching out for coyotes

 After you write your paragraph, you might want to draw an illustration. Share your paragraph and drawing with your partner. How are your animal heroes alike and different?

TAKE NOTES

Take notes and annotate as you read the passages "Armadillo: Little Armored One" and "Big Sticky Feet."

Look for an answer to the question. *How do animals' adaptations help them survive?*

_____

_____

_____

_____

_____

_____

_____

PASSAGE 1 EXPOSITORY TEXT

Armadillo:
Little Armored One

Like many tourists, the armadillo went to the state of Florida for the warm weather. This odd mammal wasn't originally from Florida. Armadillos have expanded their habitat from the southwest into this state. They continue to move north until they find the winters too cold. An armadillo's hard armor doesn't keep it very warm. Like all animals, armadillos have adapted, or changed, to survive in their environment.

Protection

Armadillos are related to sloths and anteaters. Like these animals, armadillos usually move slowly. However, they can run up to thirty miles per hour to escape from coyotes and other predators. They're also protected by an unusual feature.

The name *armadillo* comes from a Spanish word that means "little armored one." The armadillo's "armor" is made of bony plates that cover its back, legs, head, and tail. These plates are like a turtle's shell. Turtles, however, are reptiles. Armadillos are the only mammals that have this kind of bony armor.

Finding Food

Like sloths and anteaters, armadillos sleep a lot and eat insects. During the summer, they hunt at night to keep cool. Long hairs on the sides of their bellies help them feel around in the dark. They also have a good sense of smell. They search the ground for ants, beetles, and termites. They sniff and snort like a pig.

Armadillos have strong legs and huge front claws that make them very good diggers. Like anteaters and sloths, they have long, sticky tongues. This helps them reach ants, termites, and other insects that live in tunnels.

The armadillo might look strange, but its odd adaptations have helped this Florida newcomer survive!

Sean Lema/Shutterstock

TAKE NOTES

TAKE NOTES

_____

_____

_____

_____

_____

_____

_____

_____

_____

_____

_____

_____

_____

_____

_____

_____

_____

PASSAGE 2   EXPOSITORY TEXT

BIG STICKY FEET

Anole lizards are small lizards that live throughout the Caribbean islands. The lizards have special toe pads. Those are the flat, sticky bottoms of their toes. The pads stick to smooth surfaces. They help the lizards climb trees.

In 2017, the Turks and Caicos Islands were hit by two powerful hurricanes—Irma and Maria. Scientists had studied anole lizards before the hurricanes. After the hurricanes passed, scientists went to observe the lizards. Had they survived the hurricanes?

Scientists didn't know what to expect. What they found surprised them. These lizards were different. They had much larger toe pads. Their front legs were longer. The hurricanes had swept away the lizards with smaller toe pads.

The larger toe pads had given these lizards an advantage. They could hold on tightly during a hurricane. They reproduced more anole lizards with large toe pads. Their unique adaptation helped them survive on their island habitat.

COMPARE THE PASSAGES

Review your notes on "Armadillo: Little Armored One" and "Big Sticky Feet." Then create a Venn diagram. Use your notes and diagram to show how information in the passages is alike and different.

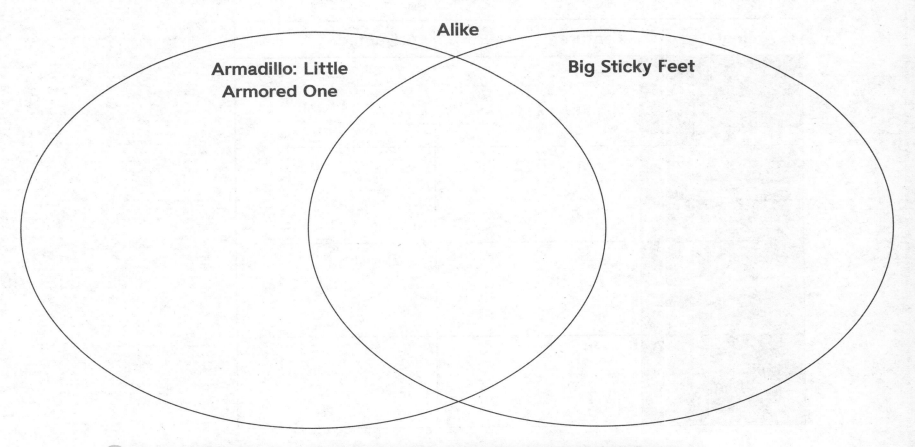

Alike

Armadillo: Little Armored One

Big Sticky Feet

Synthesize Information

Think about how the weather affected anole lizards. Imagine if armadillos continued to move north into places with colder winters. What kind of change might scientists observe in the armadillos?

CHECK IN 1 2 3 4

THE ADVANTAGES OF ADAPTATIONS

Think about the animals you have read about. What adaptation did the animal have? How did the adaptation help the animal survive? Complete the chart below.

Animal	Feature	Advantage

COLLABORATE

Choose two animals to discuss with a partner. Write about how their features give them an advantage in their environment.

_____

_____

Reflect on Your Learning

Talk About It Reflect on what you learned in this unit. Then talk with a partner about how you did.

I am really proud of how I can _____

_____

_____

_____

_____

Something I need to work more on is _____

_____

_____

_____

_____

> Share a goal you have with a partner.

My Goal Set a goal for Unit 5. In your reader's notebook, write about what you can do to get there.

Expository Writing Rubric

Score	Purpose, Focus, and Organization (4-point Rubric)	Evidence and Elaboration (4-point Rubric)	Conventions of Standard English (2-point Rubric)
4	• Stays focused on the purpose, audience, and task • States the central idea in a clear way • Uses transitional strategies, such as the use of signal, or linking, words and phrases, to show how ideas are connected • Has a logical progression of ideas • Begins with a strong introduction and ends with a conclusion	• Supports the central idea with convincing details • Has strong examples of relevant evidence, or supporting details, with references to multiple sources • Uses elaborative techniques, such as examples, definitions, and quotations from sources • Uses precise language to express ideas clearly • Uses appropriate academic and domain-specific language that matches the audience and purpose of the essay • Uses different sentence types and lengths	

Score	Purpose, Focus, and Organization (4-point Rubric)	Evidence and Elaboration (4-point Rubric)	Conventions of Standard English (2-point Rubric)
3	• Stays mostly focused on the purpose, audience, and task • States the central idea in a mostly clear way • Uses some transitional strategies, such as the use of signal, or linking, words and phrases, to show how ideas are connected • Has a mostly logical progression of ideas • Begins with an introduction and ends with a conclusion	• Supports the central idea with mostly convincing details • Has examples of relevant evidence, or supporting details, with references to multiple sources • Uses some elaborative techniques, such as examples, definitions, and quotations from sources • Uses some precise language to express ideas clearly • Uses some appropriate academic and domain-specific language that matches the audience and purpose of the essay • Uses some different sentence types and lengths	

Expository Writing Rubric

Score	Purpose, Focus, and Organization (4-point Rubric)	Evidence and Elaboration (4-point Rubric)	Conventions of Standard English (2-point Rubric)
2	• Stays somewhat focused on the purpose, audience, and task • States the central idea, but sometimes the central idea isn't clear • Uses a few transitional strategies, such as the use of signal, or linking, words and phrases, to show how ideas are connected • Has an uneven progression of ideas • Has an unsatisfactory introduction or conclusion	• Gives some very basic support of the central idea • Has unsatisfactory examples of evidence, or supporting details, with few references to multiple sources • Uses a few weak elaborative techniques • Uses imprecise or simple expression of ideas • Uses inappropriate or unsatisfactory academic and domain-specific language • Uses only simple sentences	• Shows a satisfactory understanding of grammar and spelling • Includes small errors, but no patterns of errors • Use of punctuation, capitalization, sentence structure, and spelling is satisfactory

Score	Purpose, Focus, and Organization (4-point Rubric)	Evidence and Elaboration (4-point Rubric)	Conventions of Standard English (2-point Rubric)
1	• Shows some relationship to the topic but shows little awareness of the purpose, audience, and task • Has little or no central idea • Has little or no organization • Has confusing or unclear ideas • Uses a few or no transitional strategies • Has many unrelated ideas that make the essay difficult to understand • Shows little understanding of the topic	• Gives very little support of the central idea • Has little, if any, use of sources, facts, and details • Has very little or no examples of evidence from the sources • Has little or no relevant or accurate evidence • Uses an expression of ideas that is not clear or is confusing • Inappropriate or unsatisfactory academic and domain-specific language • Uses only simple sentences	• Shows a partial understanding of grammar and spelling • Includes many errors in usage • Has an unsatisfactory use of punctuation, capitalization, sentence structure, and spelling
0			• Shows a lack of understanding of grammar and spelling • Includes serious errors, making the essay difficult to understand

Opinion Writing Rubric

Score	Purpose, Focus, and Organization (4-point Rubric)	Evidence and Elaboration (4-point Rubric)	Conventions of Standard English (2-point Rubric)
4	• Stays focused on the purpose, audience, and task • States the opinion in a clear way • Uses transitional strategies, such as the use of signal, or linking, words and phrases, to show how ideas are connected • Has a logical progression of ideas • Begins with a strong introduction and ends with a conclusion	• Supports the opinion with convincing details • Has strong examples of relevant evidence, or supporting details, with references to multiple sources • Uses elaborative techniques, such as examples, definitions, and quotations from sources • Uses precise language to express ideas clearly • Uses appropriate academic and domain-specific language that matches the audience and purpose of the essay • Uses different sentence types and lengths	

Score	Purpose, Focus, and Organization (4-point Rubric)	Evidence and Elaboration (4-point Rubric)	Conventions of Standard English (2-point Rubric)
3	• Stays mostly focused on the purpose, audience, and task • States the opinion in a mostly clear way • Uses some transitional strategies, such as the use of signal, or linking, words and phrases, to show how ideas are connected • Has a mostly logical progression of ideas • Begins with an introduction and ends with a conclusion	• Supports the opinion with mostly convincing details • Has examples of relevant evidence, or supporting details, with references to multiple sources • Uses some elaborative techniques, such as examples, definitions, and quotations from sources • Uses some precise language to express ideas clearly • Uses some appropriate academic and domain-specific language that matches the audience and purpose of the essay • Uses some different sentence types and lengths	

Opinion Writing Rubric

Score	Purpose, Focus, and Organization (4-point Rubric)	Evidence and Elaboration (4-point Rubric)	Conventions of Standard English (2-point Rubric)
2	• Stays somewhat focused on the purpose, audience, and task • States the opinion, but sometimes the opinion isn't clear • Uses a few transitional strategies, such as the use of signal, or linking, words and phrases, to show how ideas are connected • Has an uneven progression of ideas • Has an unsatisfactory introduction or conclusion	• Gives some very basic support of the opinion • Has unsatisfactory examples of evidence, or supporting details, with few references to multiple sources • Uses a few weak elaborative techniques • Uses imprecise or simple expression of ideas • Uses inappropriate or unsatisfactory academic and domain-specific language • Uses only simple sentences	• Shows a satisfactory understanding of grammar and spelling • Includes small errors, but no patterns of errors • Use of punctuation, capitalization, sentence structure, and spelling is satisfactory

Score	Purpose, Focus, and Organization (4-point Rubric)	Evidence and Elaboration (4-point Rubric)	Conventions of Standard English (2-point Rubric)
1	• Shows some relationship to the topic but shows little awareness of the purpose, audience, and task • Has little or no opinion • Has little or no organization • Has confusing or unclear ideas • Uses a few or no transitional strategies • Has many unrelated ideas that make the essay difficult to understand • Shows little understanding of the topic	• Gives very little support of the opinion • Has little, if any, use of sources, facts, and details • Has very little or no examples of evidence from the sources • Has little or no relevant or accurate evidence • Uses an expression of ideas that is not clear or is confusing • Includes inappropriate or unsatisfactory academic and domain-specific language • Uses only simple sentences	• Shows a partial understanding of grammar and spelling • Includes many errors in usage • Has an unsatisfactory use of punctuation, capitalization, sentence structure, and spelling
0			• Shows a lack of understanding of grammar and spelling • Includes serious errors, making the essay difficult to understand